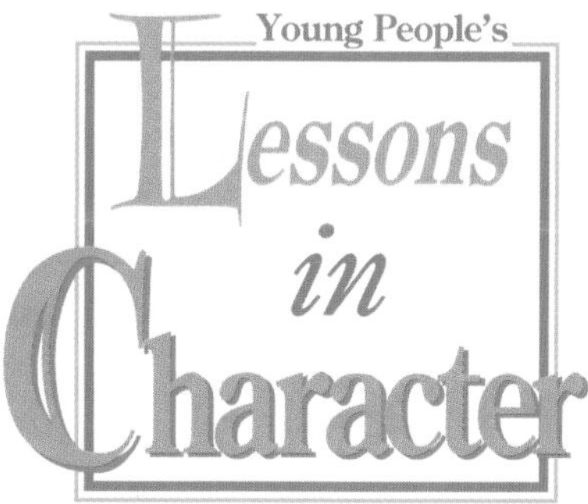

B. David Brooks, Ph.D.

Young People's Press
San Diego

Reviewers

The publisher gratefully acknowledges the efforts of the following educators, who field-tested these materials in the classroom and reviewed manuscript. Thank you for your time and insight, and for the comments from your students.

Elaine McCausland, Principal
Clare Rex, Sixth-Grade Teacher
Crafton Elementary
Pittsburgh, PA

Ms. Sharlene Linford
Supervisor, Character Education
Granite School District
Salt Lake City, UT

Emily Avegalio
Cindy Lassila
Kent Weber
McNeel Middle School
Beloit, WI

Kathy Smith, Teacher
Kennedy Junior High
Granite School District
Salt Lake City, UT

Bill Kenley, Teacher
Hunter Junior High
Granite School District
Salt Lake City, UT

Cover illustration by Eldon Doty.

Published in the United States of America.

3 4 5 6 7 8 9 — 03 02 01 00 99

ISBN 1-57279-092-X

Table of Contents

Unit Two: I Work with Numbers

I Work with Numbers

Unit Three: I Work with Words

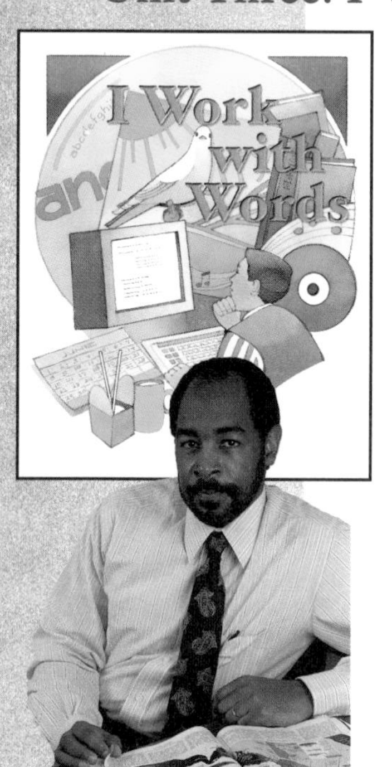
I Work with Words

Unit Four: I Work Outside

Unit Five: I Work in an Office

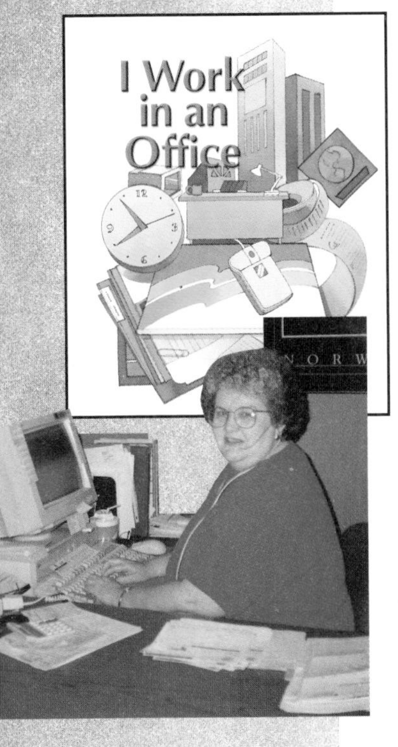

Unit Six: I Work with People

Unit Seven: I Work with Computers

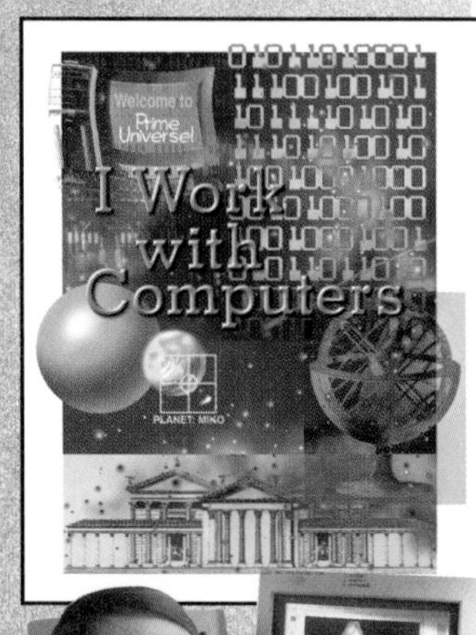

Unit Eight: I Work for the Government

Introduction

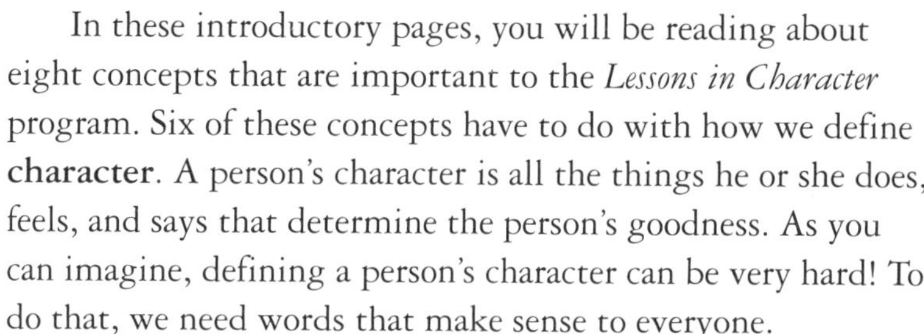

In these introductory pages, you will be reading about eight concepts that are important to the *Lessons in Character* program. Six of these concepts have to do with how we define **character**. A person's character is all the things he or she does, feels, and says that determine the person's goodness. As you can imagine, defining a person's character can be very hard! To do that, we need words that make sense to everyone.

Fortunately, in 1992, people from all walks of life who cared about character came together at a meeting in Colorado. Their goal was to choose words they could all agree on as good descriptions of character. These words are known as the *"Six Pillars of Character."** You will learn about these words in this Introduction. Then, as you read about the people who are featured in this book, you will find out which *Pillars of Character* have been most important to them in their work and in their personal lives. You can decide how you can exhibit these *"Six Pillars of Character"* in your own life.

The seventh concept you will learn about has to do with decision making and problem solving. This concept, known as STAR, can help you make wise decisions. It can help you solve problems using your best character traits. You'll see how important this concept is in the lives of the people featured in this book. This will help you realize all the ways you can use STAR in your own life.

Finally, the eighth concept is one that will help you to be a better writer. It's a process you can use to make your writing assignments as good as possible. After all, an important part of good character is being able to communicate it with others. By using the eight concepts presented in this Introduction, you will be able to TALK ABOUT (the *"Six Pillars of Character"*), THINK ABOUT (STAR), and WRITE ABOUT (the Writing Process) what is the most important part of you—your character.

**"Six Pillars of Character"* is a service mark of the Character Counts! Coalition project of the Josephson Institute of Ethics.

The *"Six Pillars of Character"*

Each word that is a *Pillar of Character* is defined below. You'll see that the Pillars are defined by people's feelings, actions, thoughts, and words. You can refer to these definitions when you read about the people featured in this book.

A trustworthy person:

- tells the truth
- stands up for what he or she believes
- shows commitment, courage, and self-discipline
- keeps his or her promises
- returns what he or she borrows
- stands by, supports, and protects family, friends, and country

A person who respects others:

- judges all people on their merits
- is courteous and polite
- appreciates and accepts people's individual differences
- accepts the right of each person to make decisions about his or her own life

RESPECT FOR OTHERS

A **responsible** person:

- thinks before acting
- considers consequences of actions on all people affected
- thinks for the long-term
- is reliable and accountable
- accepts personal responsibility
- sets a good example for others
- always tries his or her best and never gives up easily
- uses self-restraint

A **fair** person:

- treats all people fairly
- is open-minded
- listens to others
- tries to understand what others are saying and feeling
- makes decisions which affect others only after appropriate considerations

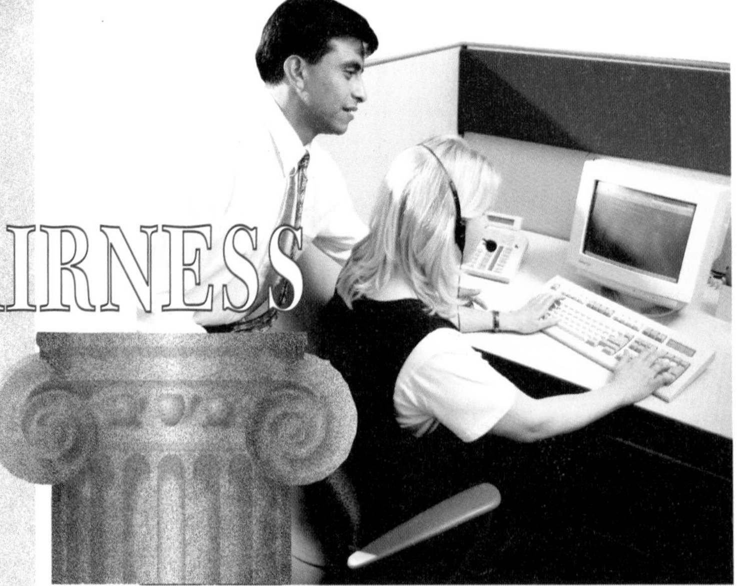

A caring person:

- is kind, caring, helpful, and compassionate
- shares with others
- treats others as he or she would like to be treated

A good citizen:

- plays by the rules
- obeys laws and respects authority
- does his or her share of the work
- stays informed
- votes
- pays taxes
- is charitable with money and time
- protects the environment and conserves natural resources

STAR

When you have an important decision to make or a problem to solve, a four-step process can help you. This process is known as STAR because the first letters of the steps spell out the word *star*:

Let's take a closer look at each step.

1. STOP

2. THINK

3. ACT

4. REVIEW

1. **Stop.** In order to solve problems, prepare for action, or make plans or a decision, you must **stop** long enough to think about what you are about to do.

---

2. **Think.** Once you **stop**, you have time to **think** so that you can make the best choice. What should you think about? Why, the ABCs of course!—the ABCs of responsible behavior, that is:

A: What are my **alternatives** or choices?

B: What is the **behavior** that I will choose?

C: What might be the **consequences** of the action I am about to take?

---

3. **Act.** Once you decide on your best choice, you must **act** upon it. Remember, *you* are making the choice here; *you* are acting; *you* are responsible for what you do. To help yourself remember this, say **I ACT** ("**I** **A**m **C**hoosing **T**o. . .").

---

4. **Review.** After taking action, **review** what happened as a result. Ask yourself:

- Did my action get me closer to or further from my goals?
- How did my action affect those around me?

What you can learn from your answers to these questions will help you with future decisions you have to make or problems you need to solve.

Next time you have a decision to make or a problem to solve, use STAR. You'll be pleased to see how it helps you.

The Writing Process

To write well, most writers follow a number of steps or stages in a process.

Prewriting In this stage you are exploring your ideas and beginning to organize them. You might:

- discuss your ideas with someone
- write your main questions about your topic
- brainstorm alone or with others
- make lists and write notes

Once you have a bank of ideas, you begin to arrange them loosely, through a further list, word cluster, or informal outline. If you are writing fiction, you may want to write brief notes about your main characters, describe or draw the setting, and make a simple plot outline (a list of what happens).

Drafting When you write your first draft, focus on getting your ideas down quickly. Refer to your prewriting as you need to. Research suggests that this stage will be more successful if you are not worried about grammar, punctuation, and spelling as you write your first draft. Think about your audience and what it is you want to say to them.

Revising Now you will take a critical look at your draft. You might pretend you have never seen it before to help you:

- look for places where you need to add details or transitions
- find details that are unnecessary and need to be deleted
- rearrange material to make it clearer or more effective
- change words and phrases to be more specific

Another very helpful phase of this step would be to show your revised draft to a classmate for a peer review.

Proofreading Now you will turn your best draft into one that contains no distracting errors. Check for:

- grammar
- punctuation
- capitalization
- spelling

Use your grammar text and dictionary as reference books. Make a final draft correcting all problems you have found.

Publishing You might "publish" your work in one of the following ways:

- illustrate it and bind it as a book
- combine it with classmates' writing and bind it as an anthology
- illustrate it and display it on a bulletin board
- read it aloud to your classmates or to a group of children

Remember that you can go back and rethink and rewrite your work. Some famous writers never feel finished and keep revising even after their work is published. As a student of writing, you also can keep working until you are satisfied.

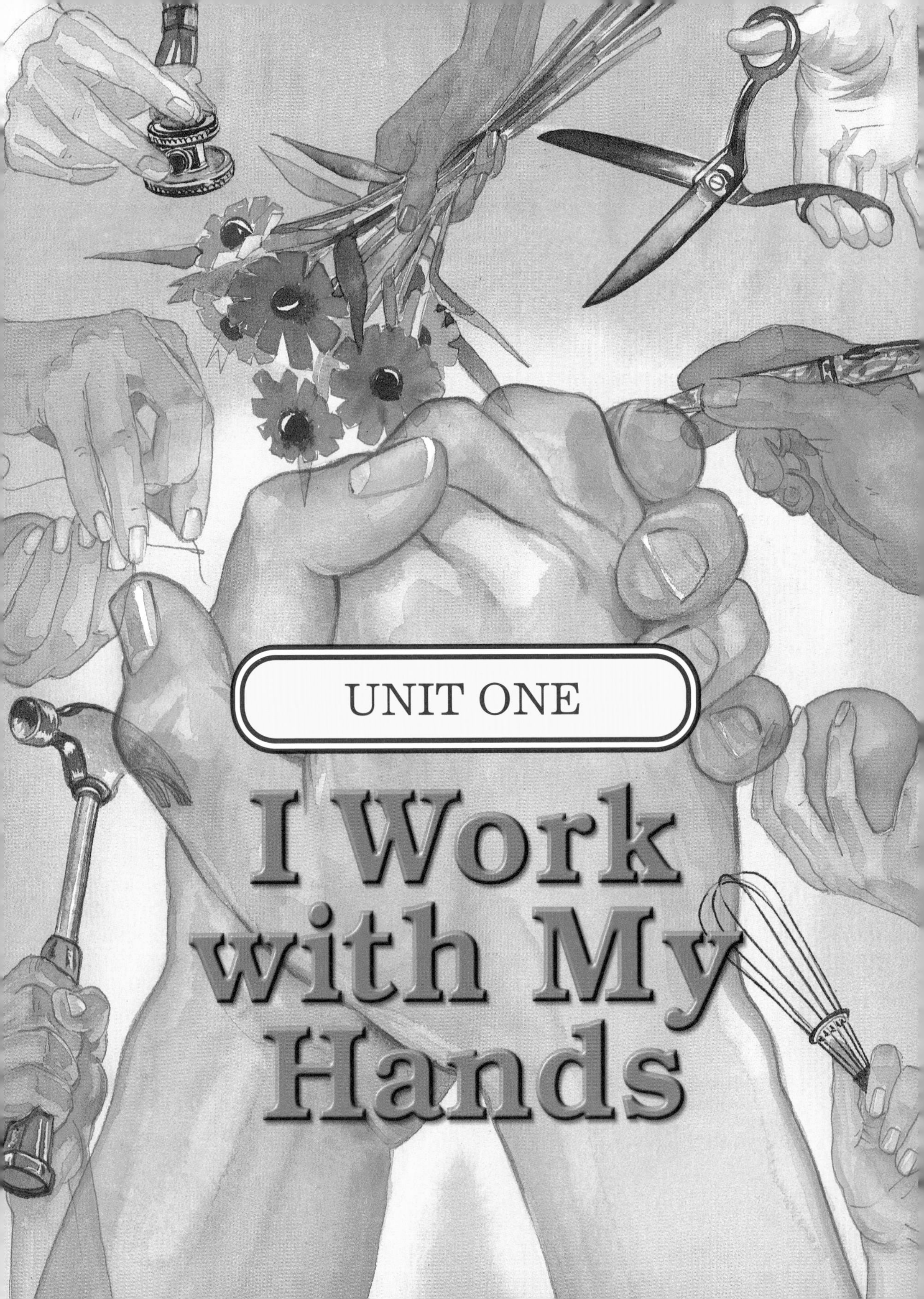
UNIT ONE
I Work with My Hands

The Village Blacksmith

by Henry Wadsworth Longfellow

Under a spreading chestnut tree
The village smithy stands;
The smith, a mighty man is he,
With large and sinewy hands;
And the muscles of his brawny arms
Are strong as iron bands.

His hair is crisp, and black, and long,
His face is like the tan;
His brow is wet with honest sweat,
He earns whate'er he can,
And looks the whole world in the face,
For he owes not any man.

Week in, week out, from morn till night,
You can hear his bellows blow;
You can hear him swing his heavy sledge,
With measured beat and slow,
Like a sexton ringing the village bell,
When the evening sun is low.

And children coming home from school
Look in at the open door;
They love to see the flaming forge,
And hear the bellows roar,
And catch the burning sparks that fly
Like chaff from a threshing floor.

He goes on Sunday to the church,
And sits among his boys;
He hears the parson pray and preach,
He hears his daughter's voice,
Singing in the village choir,
And it makes his heart rejoice.

It sounds to him like her mother's voice,
Singing in Paradise.
He needs must think of her once more,
How in the grave she lies;
And with his hard, rough hand he wipes
A tear out of his eyes.

Toiling, rejoicing, sorrowing,
Onward through life he goes;
Each morning sees some task begun,
Each evening sees it close;
Something attempted, something done,
Has earned a night's repose.

Thanks, thanks to thee, my worthy friend,
For the lesson thou has taught!
Thus at the flaming forge of life
Our fortunes must be wrought;
Thus on its sounding anvil shaped
Each burning deed and thought.

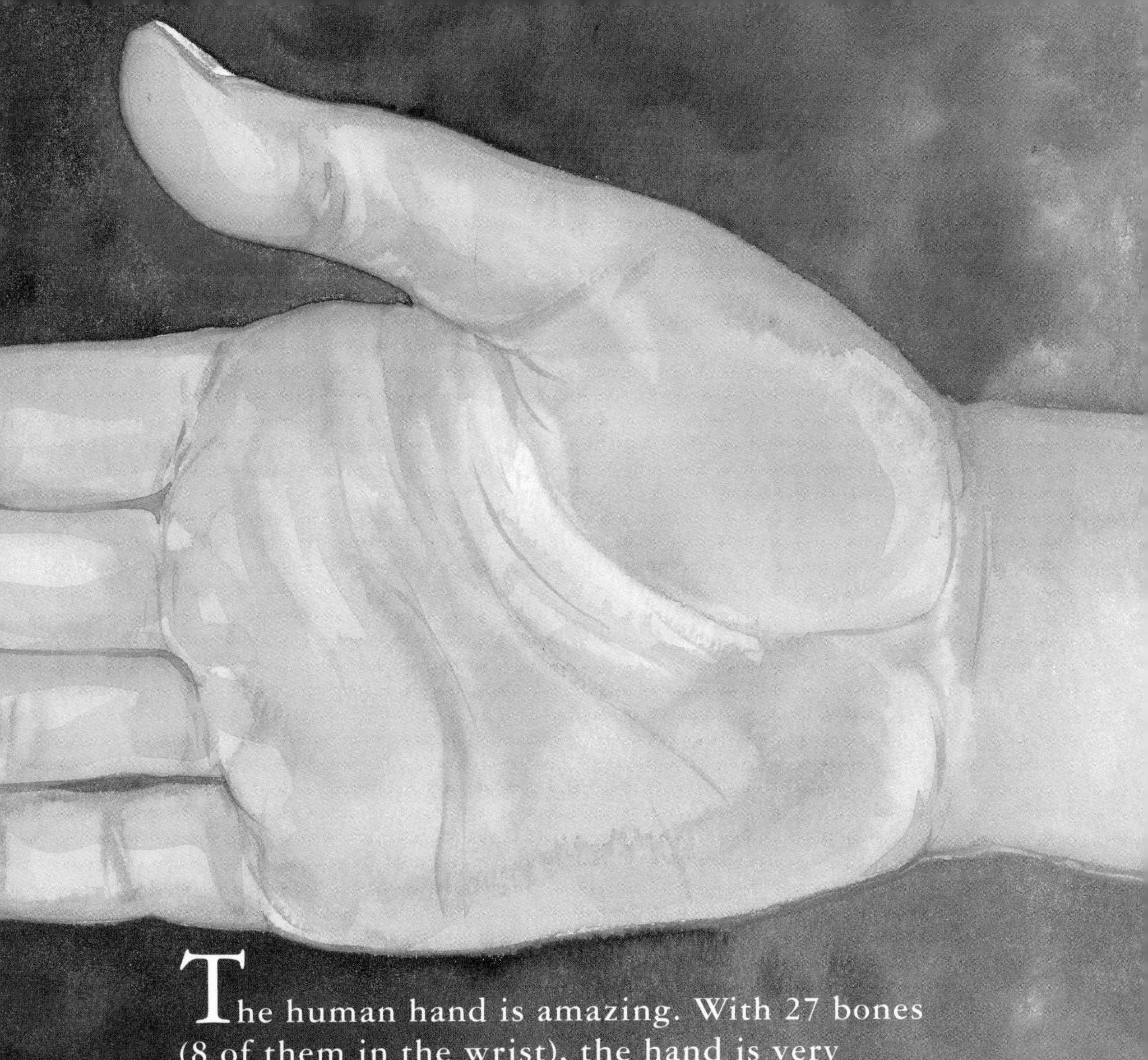

The human hand is amazing. With 27 bones (8 of them in the wrist), the hand is very flexible. Just think of the work that a hand can do! Whether it's the tough daily work of the blacksmith or his gentle touch to wipe away a tear, the hand makes it possible.

What other jobs depend on the complex work of the hand? In this unit, you'll find out about four careers in which the hand plays a crucial role. You'll read about four people who, like the blacksmith, show good character in their work, as they toil each day with their hands.

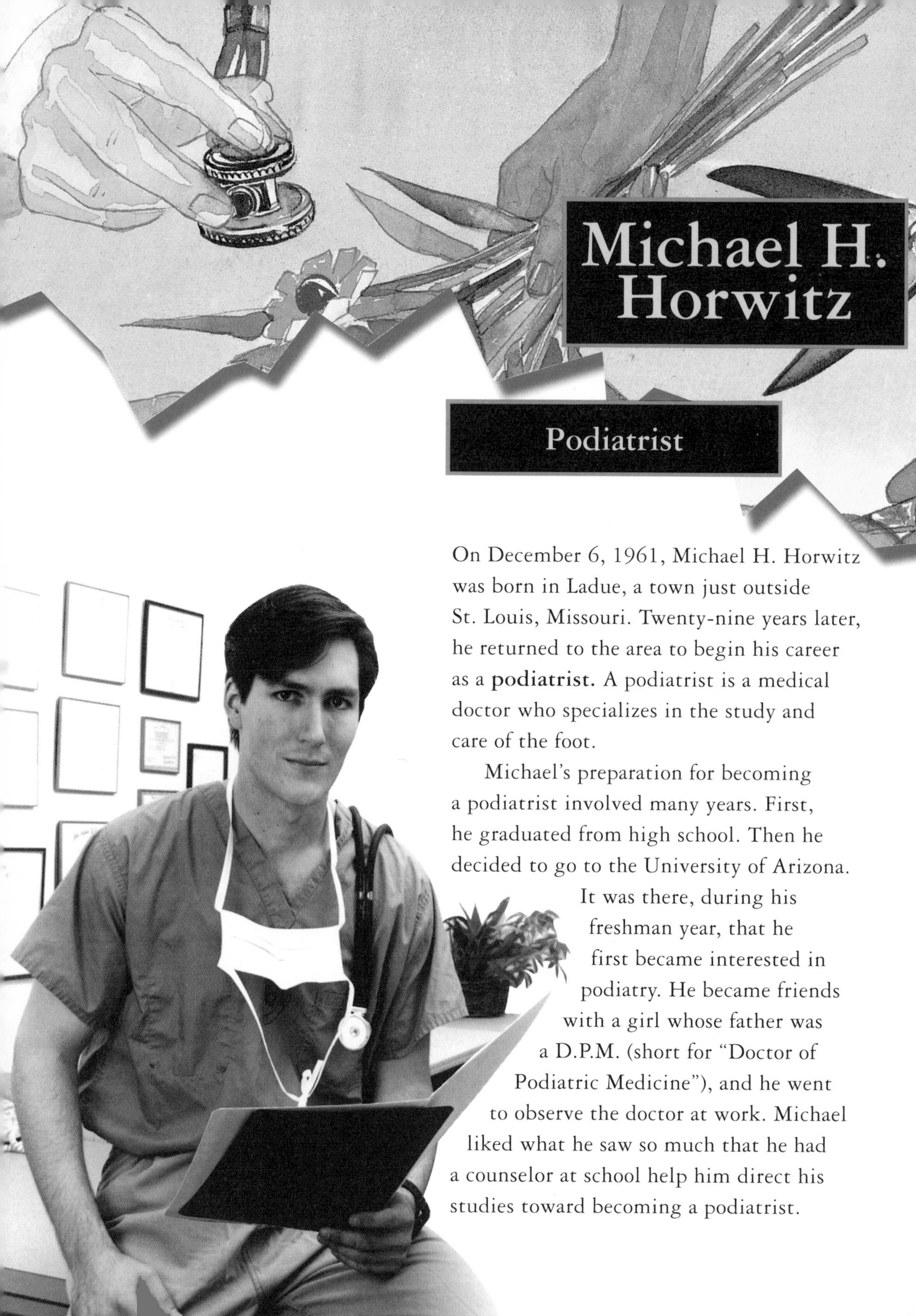

Michael H. Horwitz

Podiatrist

On December 6, 1961, Michael H. Horwitz was born in Ladue, a town just outside St. Louis, Missouri. Twenty-nine years later, he returned to the area to begin his career as a **podiatrist.** A podiatrist is a medical doctor who specializes in the study and care of the foot.

Michael's preparation for becoming a podiatrist involved many years. First, he graduated from high school. Then he decided to go to the University of Arizona. It was there, during his freshman year, that he first became interested in podiatry. He became friends with a girl whose father was a D.P.M. (short for "Doctor of Podiatric Medicine"), and he went to observe the doctor at work. Michael liked what he saw so much that he had a counselor at school help him direct his studies toward becoming a podiatrist.

After graduating from college, Michael attended four more years of school—at the Illinois College of Podiatric Medicine. During those years, he practiced the skills he was learning, working at various hospitals. By 1990, Dr. Horwitz was prepared to open his own practice.

What he was not prepared for, though, was how to answer his own questions about his profession, such as: "How do I look people in the eyes and tell them I can't treat them because they have no insurance or money to pay for even the supplies needed to make them better?" Dr. Horwitz became very sad when he realized how often he might have to ask himself this question. So, in his free time, he turned to music as a way to "keep his sanity."

> "How do I look people in the eyes and tell them I can't treat them because they have no insurance or money to pay for even the supplies needed to make them better?"

In 1995, after writing and producing pop and alternative songs for several years, Dr. Horwitz hit upon a way to use his music to help others besides himself who were worrying about the health care system. He produced an album, titled *Dangerous Ground*. The profits made from the sales of this album go to the Caring Program for Children. This program was developed in Missouri to help provide *all* children with basic health care, even when their families cannot afford to pay for it.

As a doctor who is also a musician, Michael Horwitz has found a perfect match between his interests and talents and

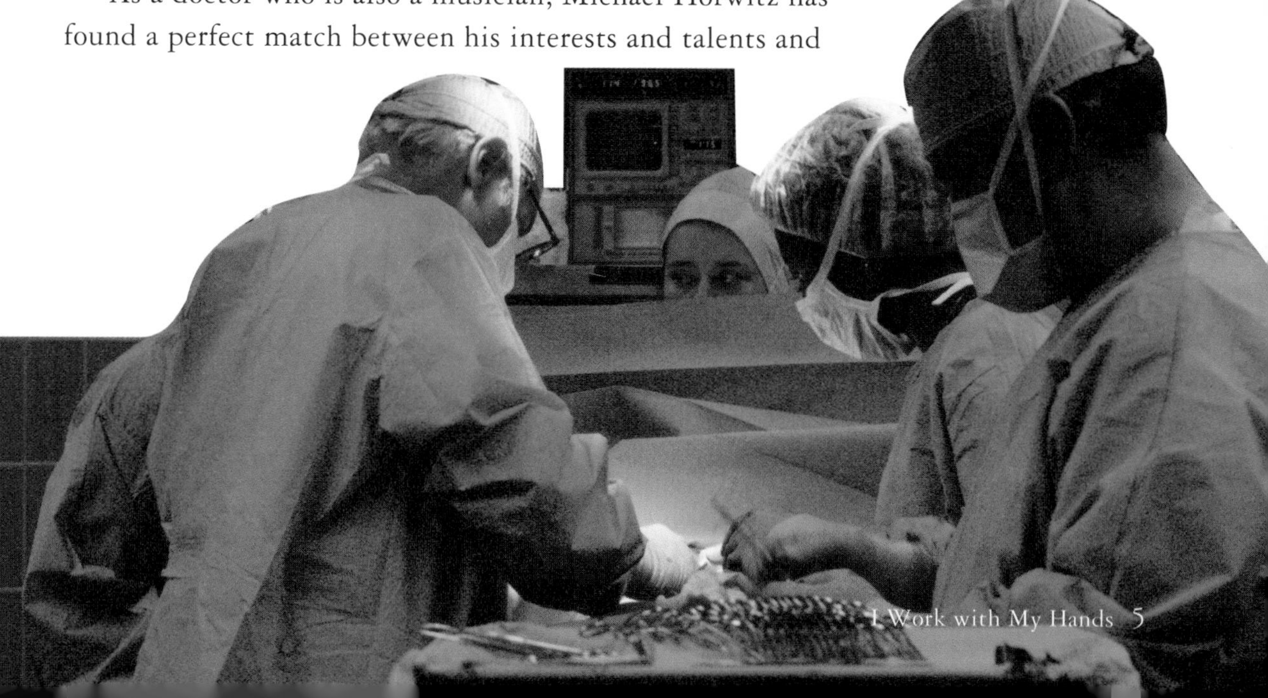

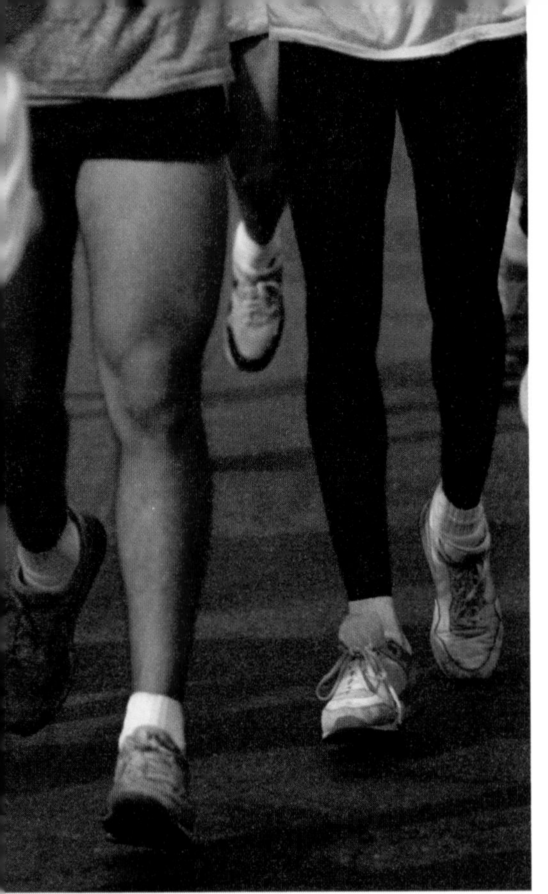

his work. His finger **dexterity** (ease of movement), honed by years of playing video games, his attraction to the sciences, and his creativity are all useful to him on the job.

Most importantly, Dr. Horwitz gets to help people. He explains that most of his patients have pain when they walk, play sports, or work. He enjoys using his skills to ease their pain as quickly as possible. When he has to, Dr. Horwitz performs **surgery,** correcting the problem through an operation.

Dr. Horwitz chooses Trustworthiness and Responsibility as the two most important Pillars of Character for him. As he says, "A patient needs to be able to *trust* my judgment and skills, and I must take full *responsibility* for my decisions and actions on behalf of the patient." And he offers these words of advice to you: "In middle school, you don't *have* to be a straight A student—I wasn't. But you do need to work hard and get your best results. When choosing a career, try to remember what activities you enjoy while at play; these activities will help you to decide the perfect career for your future."

Critical Thinking

1. How did Michael get the idea to study podiatry?
2. How does Dr. Horwitz "keep his sanity" when his work troubles him?
3. What is most important to Dr. Horwitz about his work?
4. How would you describe Dr. Horwitz's character?

Trustworthiness
Responsibility

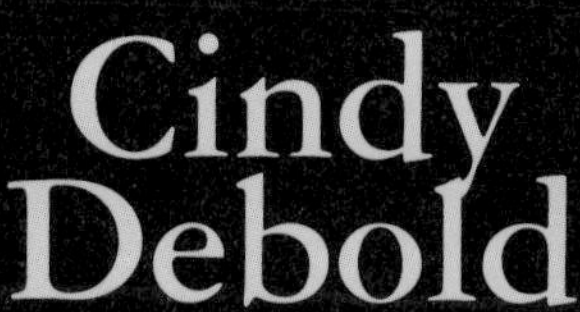

Cindy Debold

Sculptor

When she was 8 years old, Cindy Debold decided she wanted to be an artist. Her uncle was an artist, and it could have been his attitude toward her art that gave her the determination to succeed. As she says, "I got the impression that he didn't think I was a very good artist. . . I decided to show him he was wrong."

From that young age on, Cindy never changed her mind. She worked steadily to improve her knowledge and talent. She went on to earn a college degree in art. Still, it was some 30 years after her decision as an 8-year-old when she discovered the special form of art that has become her first love, sculpting. She explains: "I didn't sculpt until I moved to Austin, Texas, in 1989. After my first class my **intuition** told me this was something I would really enjoy doing the rest of my life. My hands seemed to have a **facility** for the clay media that I had not been aware of."

With her typical dedication to improvement, Cindy proceeded to find out all she could regarding sculpture. Since 1989 she has taken more than 30 classes in sculpture. She has learned about the human body's structure, and she has explored many different approaches to sculpting—carving, welding, molding clay, casting in bronze, and using plaster and concrete, to name a few.

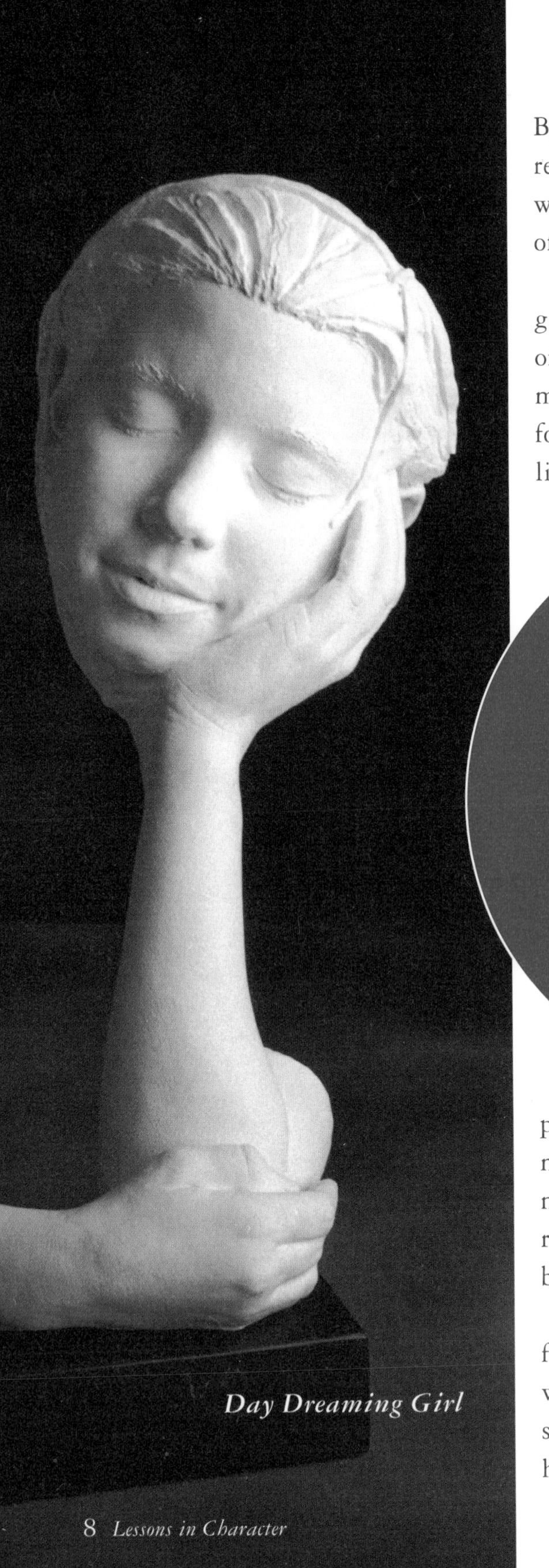

Day Dreaming Girl

By 1993 Debold had gained enough respect from her fellow sculptors that she was named president of the Texas Society of Sculptors.

Along the way Cindy Debold also has gained much recognition for a special type of sculpture—face casting. Through this method, Cindy can preserve a person's face forever. She has done casts of famous people like politicians and musicians, but the most precious casts to her are those of her family members. When she sees her father's cast next to her sons', for example, she sees resemblances that she had not noticed before on their moving faces.

Sisters

Clearly, in sculpture Cindy Debold has found her niche. She says that when she works she feels "totally absorbed" by what she's doing. Her level of concentration is high. She's a very thoughtful worker as well.

She acknowledges the importance of STAR, especially when doing molds or working in stone: "You must stop and think things through first or you might destroy your original work."

When she's not absorbed in work, Cindy is busy exploring the world. She loves to enjoy nature's beauty, experience other art forms such as dance and theater, and learn exciting new skills like how to fly an airplane. Cindy also enjoys people. She encourages you to remember a few important lessons life has taught her.

Stone Sitter

> "Don't be afraid to give honest compliments to others. It will make you feel good and others too. And don't forget to laugh! Then last but not least, I encourage you to be a volunteer. Do some work that you enjoy and that is of benefit to others."

Without a doubt, Cindy Debold gives the world much more than her sculptures. She gives the goodness of herself.

STAR

Critical Thinking

1. What first prompted Cindy to be an artist?
2. What major change occurred in Cindy's career when she was 38?
3. What does Cindy Debold value most about face casting?
4. How would you describe Cindy Debold's character?

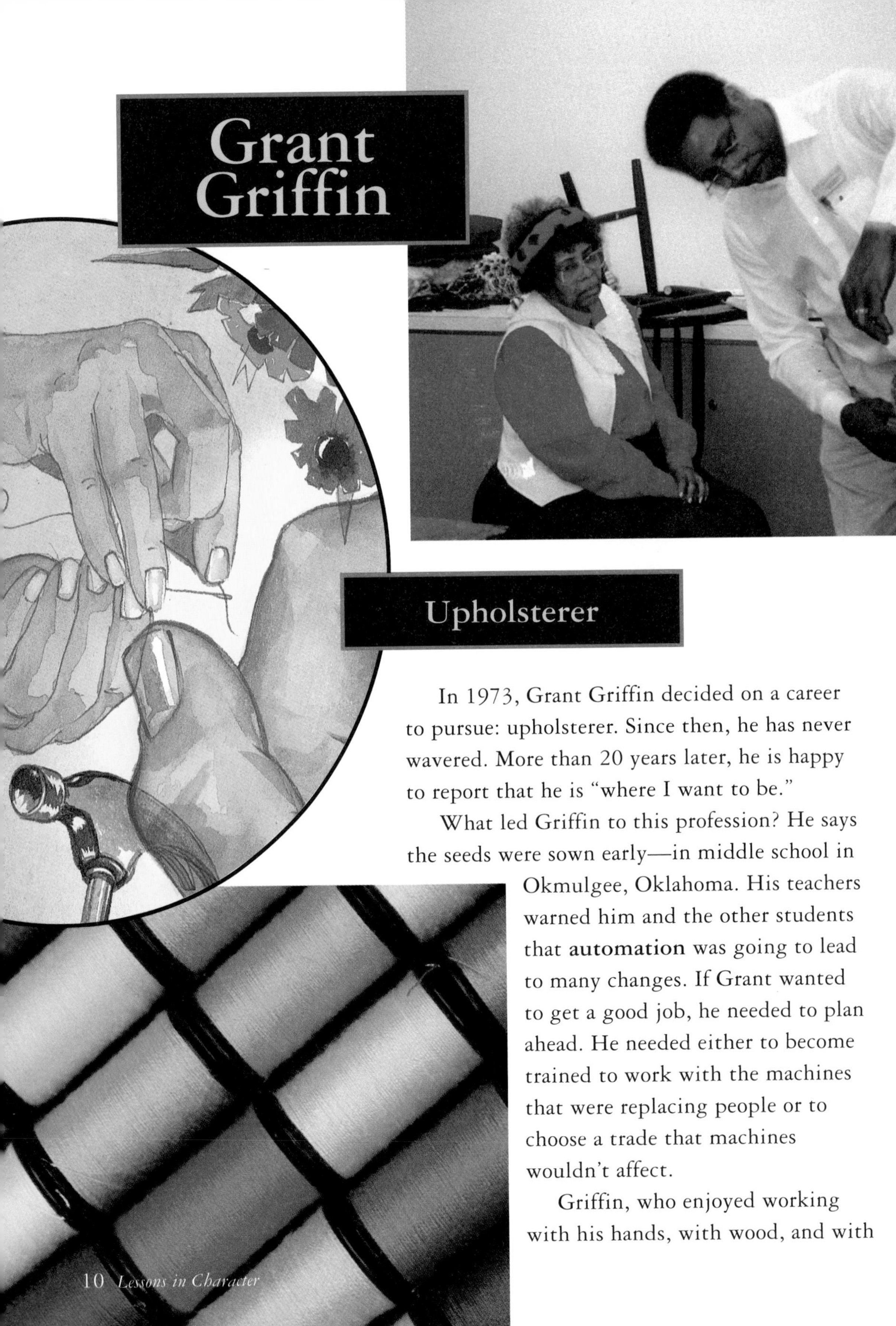

Grant Griffin

Upholsterer

In 1973, Grant Griffin decided on a career to pursue: upholsterer. Since then, he has never wavered. More than 20 years later, he is happy to report that he is "where I want to be."

What led Griffin to this profession? He says the seeds were sown early—in middle school in Okmulgee, Oklahoma. His teachers warned him and the other students that **automation** was going to lead to many changes. If Grant wanted to get a good job, he needed to plan ahead. He needed either to become trained to work with the machines that were replacing people or to choose a trade that machines wouldn't affect.

Griffin, who enjoyed working with his hands, with wood, and with

simple equipment, chose the second option. He chose to become a **craftsman,** using his hands to do the kind of work that machines don't do. He trained for two years at Oklahoma State University to become a skilled upholsterer. He then opened his own business, where he could "be his own boss." This fulfilled a personal goal, and he stayed in business for four years.

Then, in 1979, Griffin began teaching the craft of upholstery at the same school from which he graduated. He has never left. He enjoys watching his students progress from "all thumbs" to "craftsmen" under his guidance. He also enjoys the special opportunities that a job at a university can bring. For example, in 1983 Griffin was selected to be part of a team of experts that traveled to the country of Jordan to set up a program like the one he runs in Okmulgee. Griffin stayed in Jordan for six months on this assignment.

Another favorite job for Griffin was creating the world's largest teddy bear. This work was done on behalf of abused children. Imagine their smiles when they saw the huge stuffed animal!

That Grant Griffin will continue such special work seems obvious. After all, he believes very strongly in the Trustworthiness pillar, especially **integrity**. As he says, "I have always had my own identity, but I try to work with and for others, treating them the way I would like to be treated."

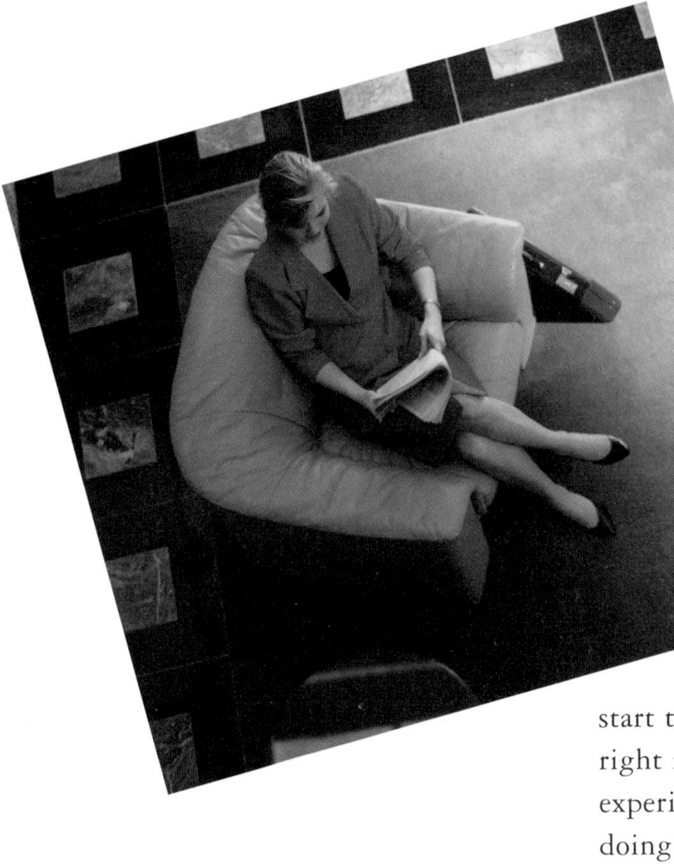

That Griffin also will continue the important work he does every day is equally obvious. When it comes to his students, he is devoted to reaching "the whole person." As their skills in the craft of upholstery grow, his students also grow as people. Griffin delights in watching a student's self-esteem and confidence blossom.

Grant Griffin encourages students your age to start thinking seriously about a career right now. In this way, you too may experience the lifelong satisfaction of doing work you love.

"I have always had my own identity, but I try to work with and for others, treating them the way I would like to be treated."

Critical Thinking

1. Why did Grant Griffin choose to be a craftsman?
2. After owning his own business, what career change did Grant Griffin make?
3. How would you describe Grant Griffin's character?
4. What does Griffin emphasize in his teaching?

Trustworthiness

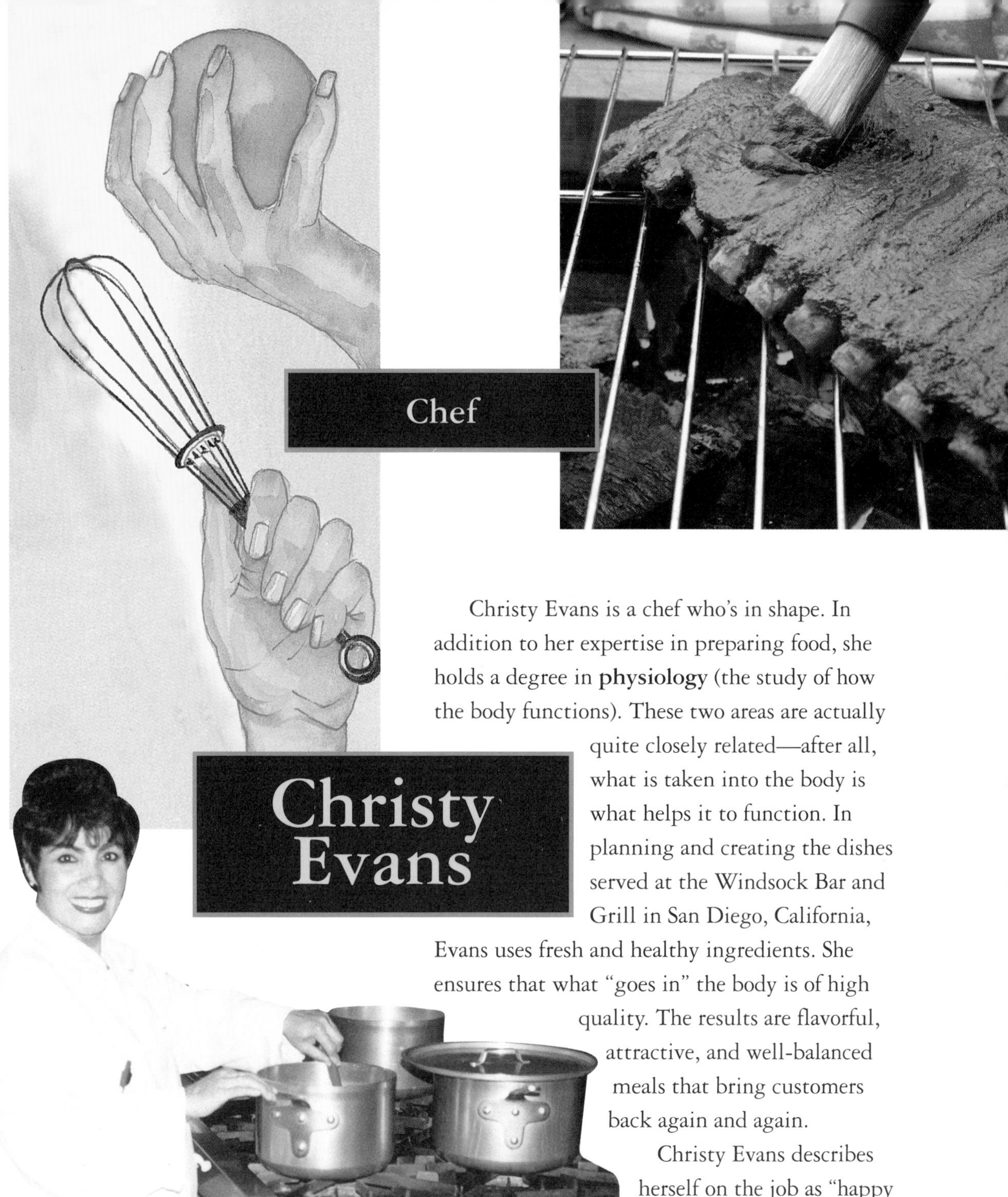

Chef

Christy Evans

Christy Evans is a chef who's in shape. In addition to her expertise in preparing food, she holds a degree in **physiology** (the study of how the body functions). These two areas are actually quite closely related—after all, what is taken into the body is what helps it to function. In planning and creating the dishes served at the Windsock Bar and Grill in San Diego, California, Evans uses fresh and healthy ingredients. She ensures that what "goes in" the body is of high quality. The results are flavorful, attractive, and well-balanced meals that bring customers back again and again.

Christy Evans describes herself on the job as "happy and good at what I do." She says her sunny attitude comes, in part, from her physical fitness. She is fit enough to run 10K races regularly, and she has won many medals and trophies for her participation. She also truly enjoys the many different aspects of her job—the creativity of designing new menu items, the possibility of meeting many new people (especially other chefs), and the actual preparation of the food.

"... being responsible helps me to achieve my goals."

Although Christy didn't formally train as a chef until after college, she says she "was born" loving to cook. In the Philippines, where she grew up, Christy loved to hang out in the kitchen and watch her mother prepare family meals. In school, she often volunteered to help in the cafeteria, and Home Economics was her favorite subject. So, when she began studying **culinary arts** under different chefs, she felt like she was coming home.

Evans credits her commitment to Responsibility for much of her success as a chef. As she says, ". . .being responsible helps me to achieve my goals and the level of excellence that puts me where I am as a chef."

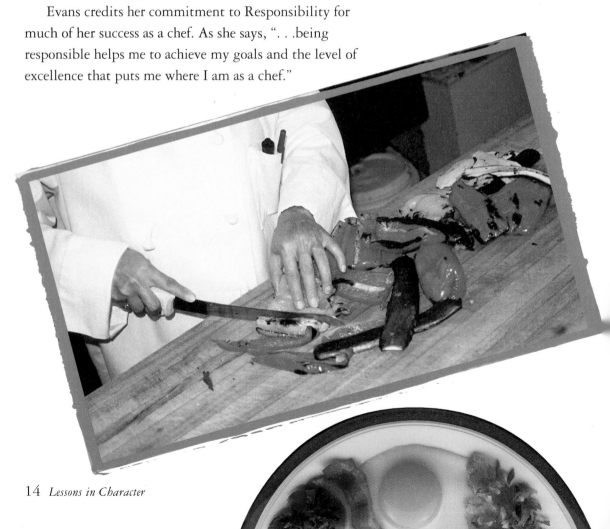

She encourages students like you to commit to responsibility in your lives:

> "Always set a good example
> for others. Be responsible.
> Don't quit or give up easily;
> set a goal and do your best."

No doubt Evans would also encourage you to take care of your physical self. Exercise, eat right, and experience the lift in health and happiness that Christy Evans has.

Critical Thinking

1. How does Christy Evans's knowledge of physiology influence her in her work as a chef?
2. How does Evans explain her positive outlook on her work?
3. What led Christy to be a chef?
4. How would you describe Christy Evans's character?

Group Project

Making a Mobile

Work with a group of four or five students to make a mobile. One purpose of this project is to experience doing work using your hands. So, as you are making your mobile, think about yourself in a career working with your hands. How do you like it? Another purpose is to make a visual illustration of the amazing abundance of career possibilities. Begin by making lists of related careers. They may be grouped around areas such as sports, media, arts, crafts, retail, food, and so on. Or perhaps you want to group them by places of work, amount of training, amount of income, or another system of your choice.

Remember to use your best character traits as you work with your group.

Materials — wire coat hangers, yarn or other cord, colored paper, markers

Method — Cut a variety of shapes from the colored paper. Write the names of various related careers at random on both sides of the paper shapes. You might want to illustrate some of the careers, or attach buttons, feathers, seeds, or other objects as decorations. Using the yarn, tie shapes with related careers to coat hangers. Then build your mobile from the bottom up. Use yarn to attach the coat hangers to each other, finding the balance point on each as you work up.

I Work with My Hands

Literature

Trades

by Amy Lowell

I want to be a carpenter,
To work all day long in clean wood,
Shaving it into little thin slivers
Which screw up into curls behind
  my plane;
Pounding square, black nails into
  white boards,
With the claws of my hammer
  glistening
Like the tongue of a snake.
I want to shingle a house,
Sitting on the ridge-pole in
  a bright breeze.
I want to put the shingles
  on neatly,
Taking great care that each is
  directly between two others.
I want my hands to have the tang of wood:
Spruce, Cedar, Cypress.
I want to draw a line on a board with a flat pencil,
And then saw along that line,
With the sweet-smelling sawdust
  piling up in a yellow
  heap at my feet.

That is the life!
Heigh-ho!
It is much easier
  than to write
  this poem.

Thinking and Journaling

This poem carries a surprise. You read it thinking how well it celebrates the work of a carpenter, and it does. The work described is not easy, especially not balancing on the ridge-pole in a breeze, nailing down shingles. There's a real sensory delight in the look and smell and feel of the wood. There's joy in the labor of creating, of constructing, of the tools of the trade.

And then you learn that Amy Lowell thinks her trade is harder than the carpenter's. She, too, deals in a kind of construction, beginning, taking away, adding to. But, heigh-ho, being a carpenter is easier.

What do you think? What's hard about each kind of work? What is glorious? Which would be more natural for you? Why do you think so? Write your thoughts and feelings in your journal.

Writing

Creative Nonfiction

Description An important new trend is emerging in writing, a new genre called creative nonfiction. It's one way of writing about your life that really "brings it to life," as if you are actually telling someone about something that happened to you. In creative nonfiction you can focus on one feeling you want your reader to understand, one triumph or trauma, one telling event.

Writers of creative nonfiction often tailor their work as they would a short story. They usually:

- Present a problem, a conflict, something that makes the reader feel some tension.
- Show an attempt or attempts to solve the problem.
- Show the resolution, if there is one.

It's important to remember that these guidelines are very loose. For example, you might be telling about a time you tried to make dinner and it turned into a gourmet feast—or a disaster.

Assignment Select an incident from your life which involved working with your hands. Remember, you are working with facts, but you are tailoring them in your own creative style, in your own voice. You can select just the details you want. You can combine events, descriptions, dialogue from more than one occasion into one story, the way that story tellers often do. Remember to follow the steps of the writing process.

PREWRITING DRAFTING REVISING PROOFREADING PUBLISHING

Purposes to entertain, to describe an event, to express feelings

Audience your classmates

My Work as a Student

Careers — Work with a partner. Each of you will choose one of the people in this unit. Review the work that each person does. Then compare their work. In what ways is it similar? In what ways is it different? (Think about training, practice, place of work, and so on.)

What are you learning at school that would help you prepare for similar careers?

Character — *Responsibility* is one character trait Dr. Horwitz stresses in his work with his hands. In what ways can you relate responsibility to your work at school? (You might think about people, property, individual and group work, learning, and so on.) List the many ways you are responsible in your life at school.

How can you tell when you are being responsible? What feelings do you feel? What thoughts do you think?

Set a goal of a new way you want to be responsible at school in the near future.

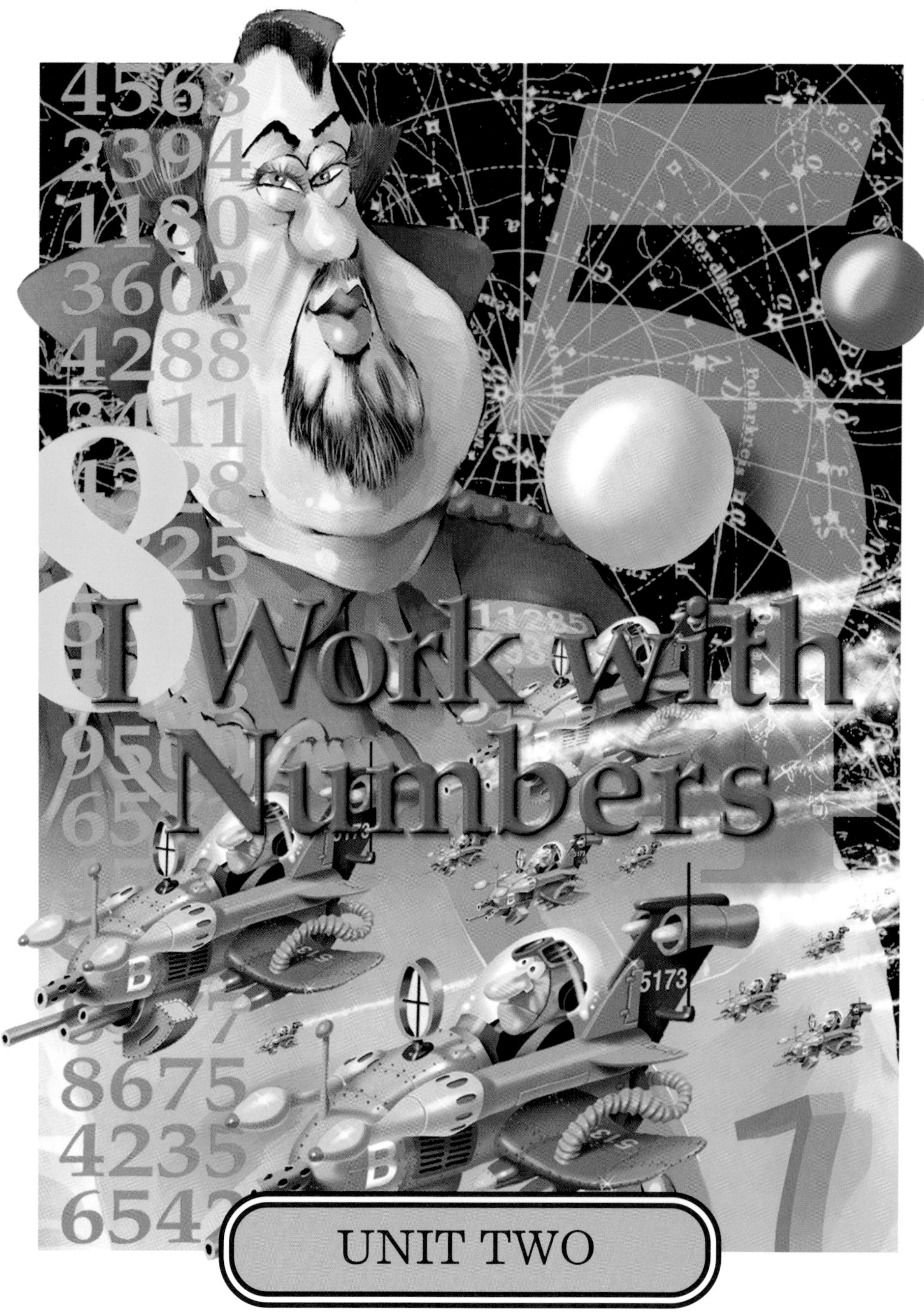
I Work with Numbers
UNIT TWO

from "The Finagle Fiasco"

by Don Sakers

This short science fiction story is about an event the main character Yagwn calls the Murphy episode. As you read, you'll see how working with numbers could have importance for the whole universe. We pick up the story as Yagwn enters his boss's office (the Grand Master of planet Euler) and greets her by saying, "How are you?"

She sighed. "I could be better, Yagwn. You've heard of this Khar-Davii, who calls himself the Conqueror? Well, it appears that he has taken over the Galactic Council. . . He has proclaimed himself Monarch of Humanity, and the inhabited worlds are falling all over their own feet to surrender to him."

I recalled hearing something about the matter on the news. "Are his weapons that formidable?"

"Apparently so. Euler is the only planet that has not yielded. I was just talking with the outlying Galactic Traffic station—Khar-Davii's fleet is even now heading toward this world." She glanced at a data screen on her desk. "Ah, excuse me. The fleet has arrived. We are surrounded."

I had no opportunity to voice an opinion. There was a bright flash of light, and suddenly the image of a corpulent human man appeared in the center of the Grand Master's office. Behind him were banks of machinery tended by warriors in full battle dress.

"I am Khar-Davii, the Conqueror. Your miserable planet has refused to accept my rule. You will surrender to me now or I will destroy your world."

I suppressed a grin; the Grand Master did not bother to hide her amusement. "I hardly think it is a miserable world. I rather like it. Conqueror, your plan of conquest would interfere with our spring term, and I'm sure that the commotion would upset many of our scholars."

Khar-Davii narrowed his brows. "As I was told—you are totally out of touch with the real universe. Mathematicians and philosophers—not a practical being in the bunch."

The Grand Master lost her smile. One thing that always bothered her was the accusation that Euler was out of touch with reality. To her, math was the highest form of reality. She stood and faced Khar-Davii.

"My dear Conqueror, I will not allow you to bother Euler. If you wish to attack, then do so—but let me show you something of our defenses first." She touched a button, and a screen behind her showed the image of a great cannon.

I drew in my breath sharply at the sight.

"And what is that machine, Grand Master?" Khar-Davii asked with a smile. "Will it shoot strings of numbers at us?"

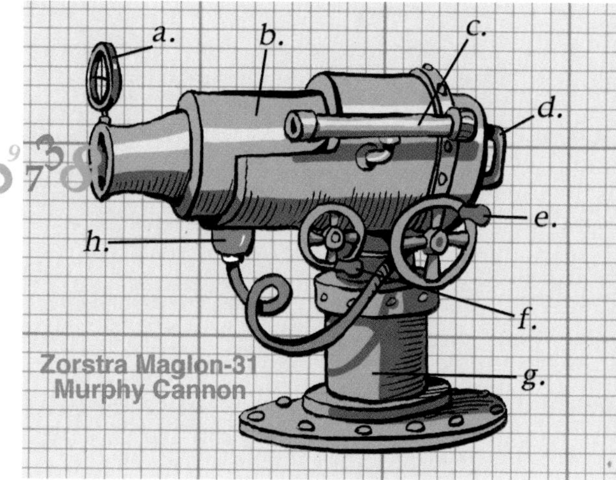

The Grand Master answered with another smile. "No doubt, Conqueror, a man with your military background has heard of the Murphy laws? That which can go wrong, will go wrong. Here we have them formulated as a theorem, and implemented as a weapon."

"And this is your defense?"

She spread her hands and regarded him as though he were a simpleton—which seemed readily apparent. "Long ago we investigated the Murphy laws completely. This machine amplifies their effects. If you attack us, your guns will fail to fire, your ships will suffer instrument breakdowns, your most trusted officers will trip and accidentally sound recall orders. You could never beat us."

Khar-Davii dissolved in a fit of laughter. "My fleet has been listening to this conversation—now they know what 'terrible weapon' Euler will use against them." He stopped chuckling. "Grand Master, prepare for your death. Fleet—Attack!"

The attack did not last long.

Since I had a little time to spare, I watched it on the viewscreens from the Grand Master's office. After twenty minutes or so, only the Conqueror's flagship was left in fighting condition. It was not too long afterward that Khar-Davii's image reappeared in the office. The Conqueror was harried and bedraggled, and there was fear in his eyes.

"Can I help you, Conqueror?" the Grand Master asked.

"Enough. Enough. Turn off that machine. We will sue for peace. I will not attack your planet any more."

"Fine." She pressed another button. "Your treaty has been logged. We have other weapons that we can use against you, should you try to break your word. I will thank you now to take the remnants of your fleet away without bothering us. . . we have important work to do."

"You will not try to prevent me from ruling the Galaxy? Your Murphy Machine is a more formidable weapon than any I possess."

She smiled. "Poor, poor Conqueror. You should have taken more mathematics classes. Deductive reasoning would have helped you. The Murphy Machine worked perfectly—as soon as it was turned on, things started to go wrong. The first problem that developed was the failure of the machine itself."

"Failure. . .?"

"Yes." She laughed. "It was the superstition of your crews that defeated you, Khar-Davii. They believed that they could not win, and so they did not."

Khar-Davii snarled, and his image vanished. Viewscreens showed his ships limping away from Euler.

RBD<22.5M
6778.WAD.QT55.8
PB.DAFCOM.ACKNOWLEDGE SIMCAR.33
MA00.666666666666.45.T
LEXON#77.3>>>>>>>>>

DATE: 66-3-24
TIME: 23:40:34HRS.
TO: ALL DISTRICT COMMANDERS AND XR OFFICERS
FROM: DATCOM.33
SUBJECT: ENDING OF HOSTILITIES

EFFECTIVE IMMEDIATELY THERE IS TO BE A CEASE FIRE WITH ALL HOSTILE UNITS OF THE GALACTIC COUNCIL. RULES OF ENGAGEMENT SHALL BE DOWNSHIFTED TO LEVEL 3-B. UNITS ARE PERMITTED TO USE DEADLY FORCE ONLY IN THE EVENT THEY ARE FIRED UPON OR GALACTIC FORCES ENTER INTO THREATENING OPERA

Was it the Grand Master's knowledge of numbers that saved her planet? Or was it her courage and wisdom?

As you study this unit you will meet four people who, like the Grand Master, have both an understanding of numbers and the good character to use their knowledge well. As you read about these people, think of other interesting jobs that involve working with numbers. In today's world, it's no science fiction that mathematicians can help us understand the universe and save lives on Earth.

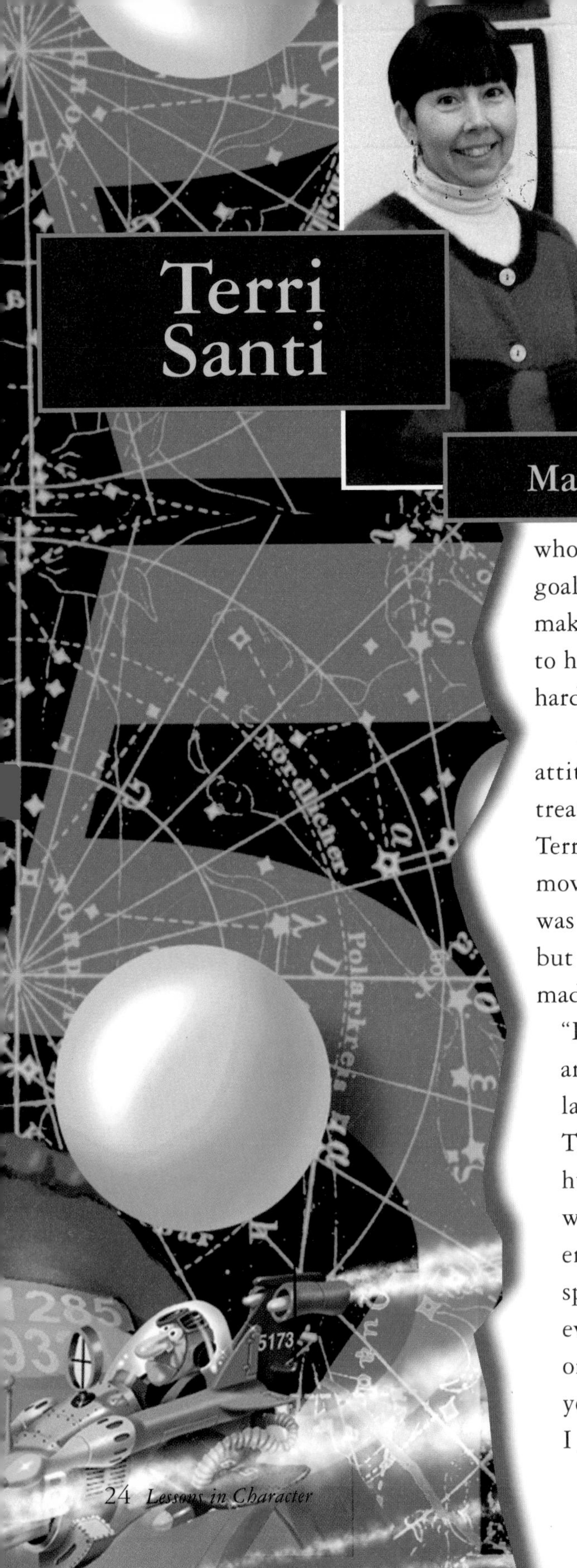

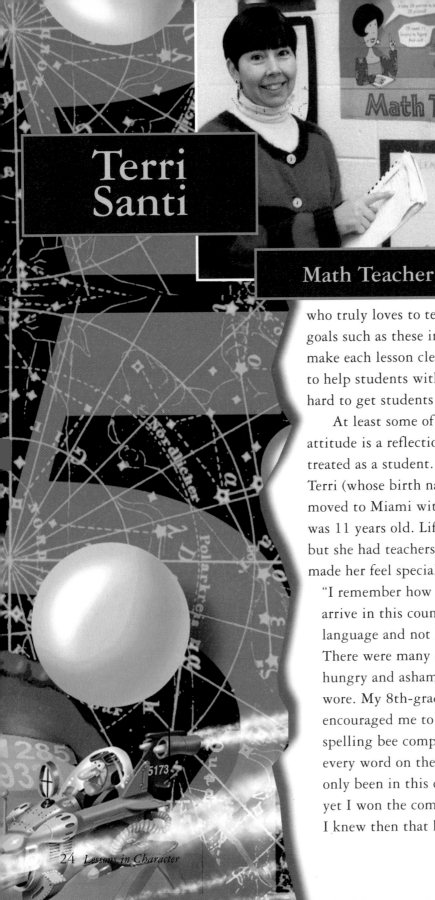

Terri Santi

Math Teacher

If you attended DeWitt Middle School in Ithaca, New York, you would be very fortunate indeed to have Ms. Terri Santi as your math teacher. She is an educator who truly loves to teach and who has personal goals such as these in her classroom: "I try to make each lesson clear and interesting. I try to help students with their problems. I try hard to get students to be independent."

At least some of Ms. Santi's caring attitude is a reflection of the way she was treated as a student. Born in Havana, Cuba, Terri (whose birth name is Olga Teresita) moved to Miami with her family when she was 11 years old. Life was not easy for her, but she had teachers who encouraged her and made her feel special. As she says:

> "I remember how difficult it was to arrive in this country not knowing the language and not having any money. There were many days when I was hungry and ashamed of the clothing I wore. My 8th-grade teacher, Mr. Garner, encouraged me to try out for my school's spelling bee competition. I memorized every word on the list he gave me. I had only been in this country two years and yet I won the competition for my school. I knew then that hard work pays off."

Terri's hard work continued as she completed high school with a straight A average. Then she went on to college. She took many education classes and practiced teaching school in Florida. She decided to concentrate on math education because, "So many people have trouble learning math." However, she also has a **masters degree** in reading education, which required hours of work beyond her college degree.

Ms. Santi's work didn't stop when her teaching career started, however. She feels that teaching is an ongoing learning experience for her. She is always preparing, always looking for that happy moment when students succeed. She loves the smile on a student's face that says, "I understand what you're saying!"

Which *Pillars of Character* does Ms. Santi credit for helping her reach her career goals? She lists Responsibility first, because she has always tried her hardest.

Next she places Citizenship, because she respects so highly the values of the United States that offered her **refugee** family a home. She is quick to remind us all what we often forget: "In spite of problems that we must all work together to solve, this is the greatest country in the world."

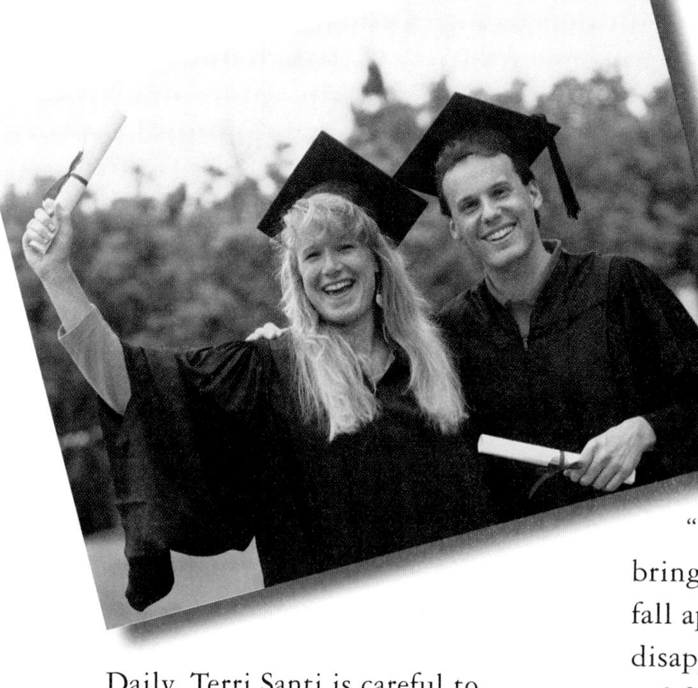

Daily, Terri Santi is careful to display the character trait of Fairness. She points out that keeping promises is very important in teaching. She knows that her students must be able to trust her so she tries to be fair to all.

And what advice does Ms. Santi give students like you? This could be summed up in "Four Rules for Life":

1. Stay away from any "friends" who truly don't care about you.
2. Stay away from drugs.
3. Work hard in school and believe in yourself.
4. Set goals that match your dreams.

When speaking from the heart, though, Ms. Santi gives advice that goes much deeper than any rules:

"You never know what life will bring you. Sometimes your plans will fall apart and other people will disappoint you. Don't grow bitter. Be sad for a while, but then smile and move on. You're in this world not just to do great things in your career but also to do great things as a human being. I tell my students: 'Whatever greatness you achieve, it is nothing, if inside you are not at peace with yourself.' "

Responsibility
Citizenship
Fairness

Critical Thinking

1. How did Terri first learn that hard work pays off?
2. In what ways does Terri's life show her commitment to hard work?
3. Why did Terri choose a career that involves numbers?
4. How would you describe Terri Santi's character?

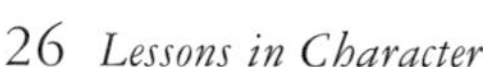

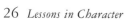

Priscilla Boyles

Insurance Agent

Since 1979, Priscilla Boyles has been busy building a career in **insurance.** It is a complicated profession. A person buys insurance from a company that promises to pay money to him or her if some sort of loss occurs in the person's life. (Examples are car crashes, fire, theft, and death of another person.)

Often, Boyles's life has been a balancing act. As a single mom, she has had to balance work and home. As an insurance agent, she has had to balance her customers' needs and the different types of plans she offers them. She must work with the customer when a loss does occur, sometimes in sad situations.

Through it all, however, Boyles has been able to make things work. As she says, "Being flexible is an important part of my career development." Boyles also has a knack for solving conflicts effectively, which helps keep things in balance. She says about the STAR model:

"This could serve as a creed in operating my business. It would encourage me to pause and reflect."

Constant preparation and education also have been keys to Priscilla Boyles's success. As a speechmaker noted when presenting an award to Boyles in 1994, Priscilla is admired for her "zeal to always increase and strengthen her professional knowledge." Steadily, she has taken course after course, passing increasingly difficult tests to become **certified** (able to work) in many areas of expertise. Because she owns her own business, Fleming Insurance Agency, it is *her* desire to keep improving that has driven her. As she says, "Self-employment requires independence and a commitment to being self-directed."

People describe Priscilla as a generous friend with a "sparkling personality." This seems to fit well with her choice of the most important *Pillar of Character*: Caring. Boyles feels that caring is

vital in all aspects of life. She says, "Caring affects my personal satisfaction and the quality of my work."

Boyles will no doubt continue to gain recognition and awards. On January 1, 1998, when she becomes president of her state's independent insurance agents association, she will be the first female president of a major insurance trade association in West Virginia history. She clearly has taken her advice to you to heart: "Enjoy yourselves. Be open to learning a variety of things. Don't limit yourself."

"Self-employment requires independence and a commitment to being self-directed."

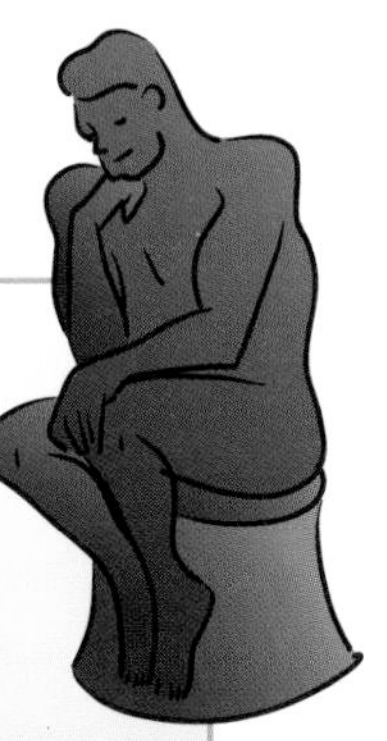

Critical Thinking

1. How is Priscilla Boyles's life like a balancing act?
2. In what way would using the STAR model help in Priscilla's business?
3. How has Boyles continued her education?
4. How would you describe Priscilla Boyles's character?

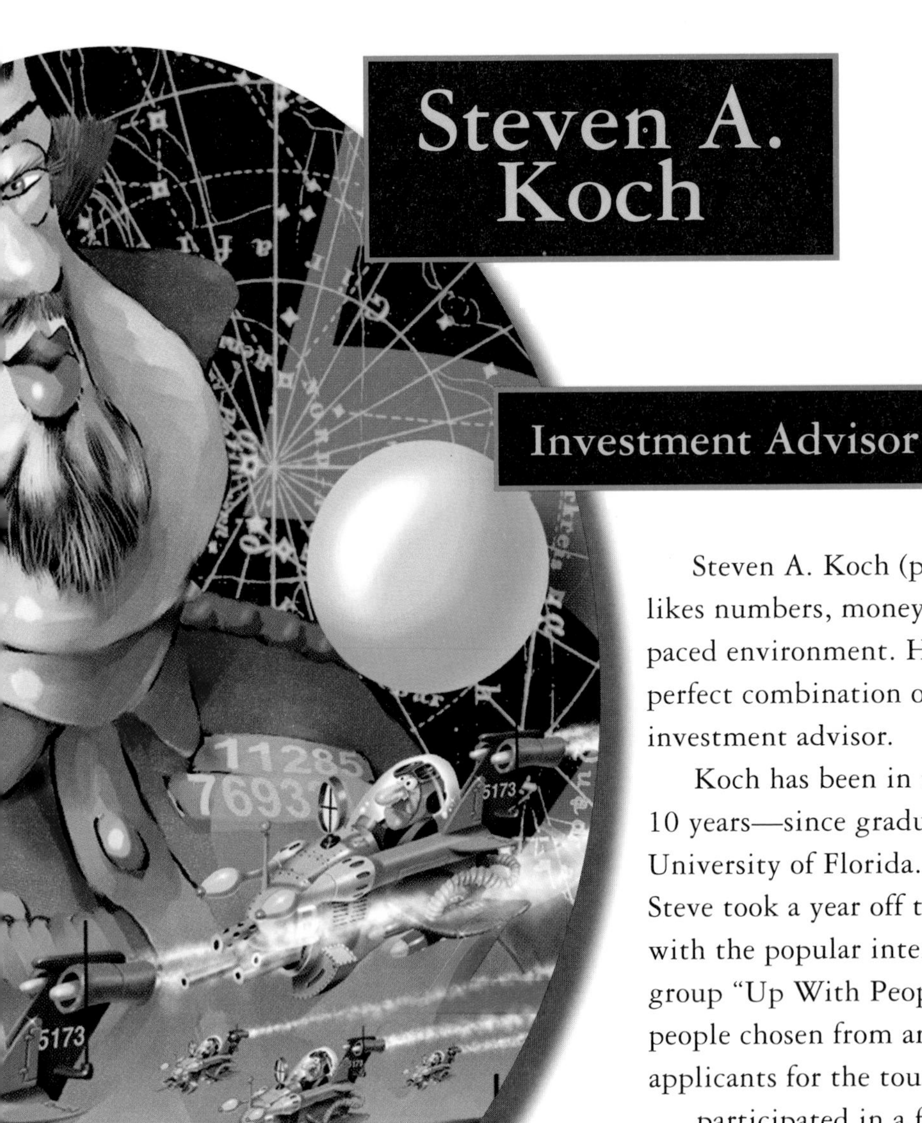

Steven A. Koch

Investment Advisor

Steven A. Koch (pronounced "cook") likes numbers, money, people, and a fast-paced environment. He has found the perfect combination of these things as an investment advisor.

Koch has been in this line of work for 10 years—since graduating from the University of Florida. While in college, Steve took a year off to do a one-year tour with the popular international singing group "Up With People." As one of 500 people chosen from among some 15,000 applicants for the tour, Koch truly participated in a fabulous experience. His life continues to be exhilarating today, however, in his chosen line of work. We can see this in the way he describes the most enjoyable aspects of his job:

> “. . . really making a difference in someone’s life with good investments—for example, helping secure a lifetime of worry-free retirement, or helping people be able to pay for a child’s or grandchild’s college education.”

“People need to know that you’re honest and that you put their needs in front of yours.”

Koch stays on top of the investment scene through research and constant attention to what is happening in the financial community. He also spends time really getting to know his clients and their goals regarding money. As he says, “Each client is an individual and must be treated as such to satisfy their unique needs.”

Building sincere relationships, working his hardest, and giving his best advice are all important parts of Steve’s commitment to Trustworthiness. This character trait seems essential to have when you are dealing with other people’s money. As Steve comments:

> “People need to know that you’re honest and that you put their needs in front of yours. Above all, they need to know they can count on you to do what you say you’ll do.”

Steve Koch's selection as a member of his company's 1997 Chairman's Council proves that his character and hard work are real. This designation by Raymond James & Associates (in St. Petersburg, Florida) is reserved for an **elite** group of advisors who "display exemplary professional growth and adherence to the highest standards of service."

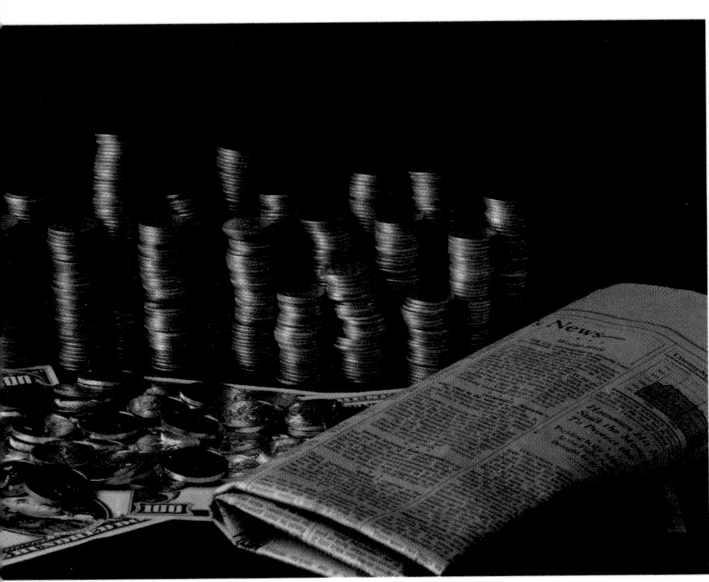

What can students like you do to start now down the road to success? Koch offers this advice: "Get the best education possible. Work is very competitive. Don't goof off too much in school, and always be careful about other people's feelings." In regard to your future investments, perhaps you should consider these golden words from Koch: "One of the best ways to begin making money is to take steps designed to prevent the loss of money." For you, that probably best translates to "Stay in school."

Critical Thinking

1. What are the most enjoyable aspects of being an investment advisor for Steven?
2. How does Koch stay current in his field?
3. How would you describe Steven Koch's character?
4. What advice does Steven give you about school?

Trustworthiness

Margaret Vazquez

Cashier

Think of your family's favorite store or restaurant, gas station or laundromat. What brings you back there again and again? Is it the **merchandise,** the prices, the location? Or could it be the friendly people who work there, who recognize you and greet you with a smile?

For those who shop at David Berkley, a specialty foods grocery in Sacramento, California, the special merchandise is certainly one reason why they keep coming back. But another reason is the people who work there—people like Margaret Vazquez, a cashier. With 15 years' experience as a cashier, Vazquez knows her job and is very good at it. Yet, what she finds most enjoyable is "the pleasure of meeting so many people."

"Be patient and choose the best alternatives."

Working with people is indeed a big part of Margaret's job. As she explains, "Cashiers must be social, quick, open-minded (able to accept all types of people), and have an outgoing personality."

Equally important, however, is a cashier's skill with numbers. At the end of a shift, a cashier's drawer must have the right amount of money in it. It's on those rare occasions when mistakes are made that a cashier's day-to-day character becomes especially important. As Vazquez says, "Cashiers handle large amounts of cash; it is important to be trusted." And what leads to trust? As Vazquez states simply: Trustworthiness.

Margaret Vazquez uses the term *fast-paced* to describe her work. This would also describe her favorite sport—ice hockey! Yet, she would caution you against a fast-paced life right now. Instead, she offers you this advice: "Be patient and choose the best alternatives." Margaret herself completed high school and two years of college, got married and started a family, before choosing her career. The result is a job that matches her natural abilities, a job in which she is very happy.

Critical Thinking

1. What does Margaret enjoy most in her work as a cashier?
2. Why are people skills so important in Margaret's work?
3. Why is it so important for Margaret to have good number skills in her work?
4. How would you describe Margaret Vazquez's character?

Trustworthiness

Group Project

Making a Scale Model

Work with a group of four or five students to make a scale model—of your school building, classroom, playing field, desk and chair, hallway with lockers, or something else. As a group, come up with a project that is both fun and manageable. Materials and time will be factors as you decide what you can actually measure and reproduce as a scale model.

Remember to use your best character traits as you work with your group.

Materials — tape measures, yardsticks, rulers, pencil and paper, assorted model materials such as craft sticks, glue, toothpicks, clay, construction paper, tape, markers

Method — Carefully take measurements of the place or object you have chosen. Decide the basic size you want your model to be. Use your best math skills to come up with an appropriate scale to use (for example, for a chair that is 36 inches high, you could use the scale 1/6 to build a model 6 inches high). Round off numbers to make your calculations easier. Another approach would be to use a box that is the approximate shape of your classroom, remove the top and one side of the box, and draw in chalkboards to scale, build representative furniture to scale, and so on. One purpose of this project is to experience working with numbers, so as you work, reflect on your thoughts and feelings.

I Work with Numbers

Literature

Arithmetic

Carl Sandburg

Arithmetic is where numbers fly like pigeons in and
out of your head.
Arithmetic tells you how many you lose or win if you know how many
you had before you lost or won.
Arithmetic is seven eleven all good children go to heaven—or five six
bundle of sticks.
Arithmetic is numbers you squeeze from your head to your hand to
your pencil to your paper till you get the answer.
Arithmetic is where the answer is right and everything is nice and you
can look out of the window and see the blue sky—or the answer is
wrong and you have to start all over again and try again and see
how it comes out this time.
If you take a number and double it and double it again and then
double it a few more times, the number gets bigger and bigger and
goes higher and higher and only arithmetic can tell you what the
number is when you decide to quit doubling.
Arithmetic is where you have to multiply—and you carry the multiplication
table in your head and hope you won't lose it.
If you have two animal crackers, one good and one bad, and you eat one
and a striped zebra with streaks all over him eats the other, how many
animal crackers will you have if somebody offers you five six seven and
you say No no no and you say Nay nay nay and you say Nix nix nix?
If you ask your mother for one fried egg for breakfast and she gives
you two fried eggs and you eat both of them, who is better in
arithmetic, you or your mother?

Thinking and Journaling

Sandburg is playing with his childhood memories of arithmetic. He reminds us of children's games and chants, as well as the burden of remembering multiplication tables. It seems as if he liked studying math but had a hard time with some of it. For his career Sandburg chose to be a writer: a journalist, historian, poet, and biographer.

But maybe you would like a career where you work with numbers. Which career might you love most? What would you love about it? What might be some drawbacks? Write your thoughts and feelings in your journal.

By the way, if you ate the two fried eggs, who is better in arithmetic?

Writing

Word Problems

Description Please look at your math books and find examples of word problems. What features do the problems have? For example, you will probably find believable situations in which people need to use math skills to solve a problem. Often the problem begins with the name of the person and a description of what he or she is trying to do. You will find facts and figures that help you understand what is needed. These will be woven into the "story" in a way that is realistic and interesting. The problem may end with a question for you to answer using your math skills. Or it may end with instructions about something you are to do.

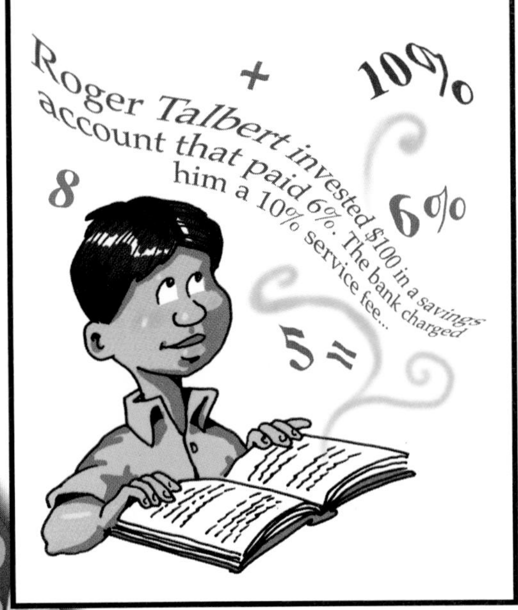

Word problems in math usually:

- Describe a realistic situation.
- Contain all the figures and facts you need.
- Don't contain any unnecessary information.

Assignment Using the writing process, write a word problem that requires the reader to use the skills you are studying now in math. You may choose to model your problem on one or more in your math book, but you must do more than change the names and numbers! You need to come up with a similar situation, but not a duplication. The main danger is that you will leave out a fact or figure that is essential. During the revising step, as you edit your problem, pretend you have never seen it before. Go through it systematically, making sure every needed bit of information is present. Then exchange word problems with a classmate and check to be sure they are solvable.

PREWRITING DRAFTING REVISING PROOFREADING PUBLISHING

Purposes to examine word problems, to write a word problem

Audience your classmates

My Work as a Student

Pair Share

Careers — Work with a partner. Each of you will choose one of the people in this unit. Review the work that each person does. Then compare their work. In what ways is it similar? In what ways is it different? (Think about training, practice, place of work, and so on.)

What are you learning at school that would help you prepare for similar careers?

Character — *Caring* is a character trait Priscilla Boyles emphasizes in her work as an insurance agent. In what ways can you relate caring to your work at school? (You might consider the ways you show you care about others through sharing, feeling empathy, helping, listening, and talking.)

List the many ways you are caring in your life at school.

How can you tell when you are being a caring person? What feelings do you feel? What thoughts do you think?

Set a goal of a new way you can be more caring at school in the near future.

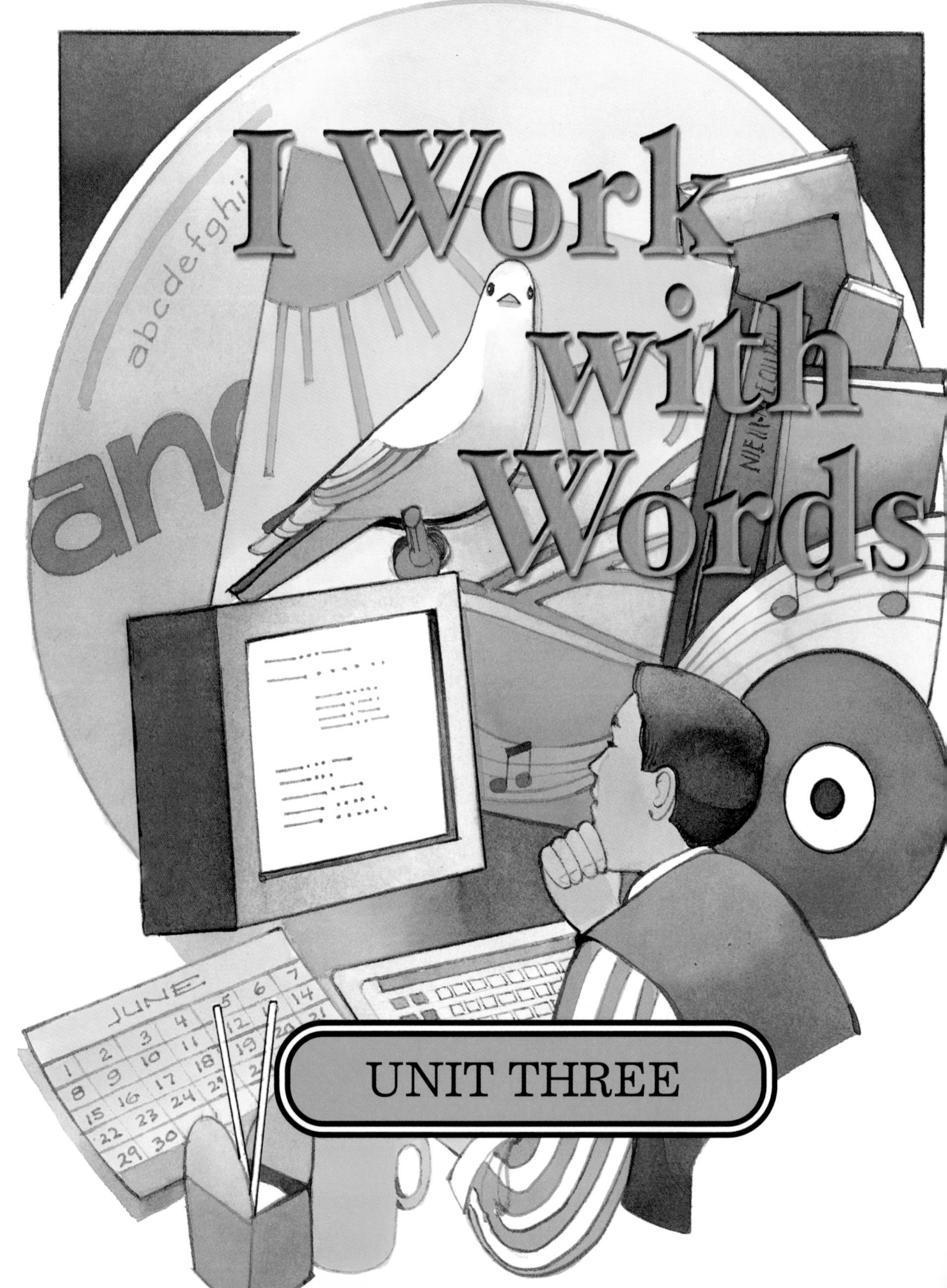
I Work with Words
UNIT THREE
abcdefghi
JUNE

Freedom *by Wimal Dissanayake*

Words, one by one
arrive on the empty page
like honored guests.
Ordered thoughts move
gracefully.
Outside the window,
on the sill,
I see the figure of a bird,
sun on its feathers—
a brownish, medium-sized bird.
I try to wave it away,
but it intrudes more stubbornly.
It has a quizzical look in its eye.
Ignoring its rude presence
I try to compose my lines,
but I feel uneasy
being observed by a brownish,
medium-sized bird
with sun on its feathers—

What is the freedom this poet from Sri Lanka writes about? Is it the freedom he feels when he is able to do what he loves—work with words without interruption? Or is he writing about the bird's freedom to be outside in the sun?

If you enjoy puzzling through questions like these, you might enjoy a career that would allow you to work with words. You probably understand Dissanayake's delight in filling the page with words and his self-discipline in working steadily to write.

As you study this unit, you will meet four people who work with words every day. You will see that working with words goes beyond loving to read, write, speak, and listen. It includes having the good character to work hard, stay focused, and use words fairly.

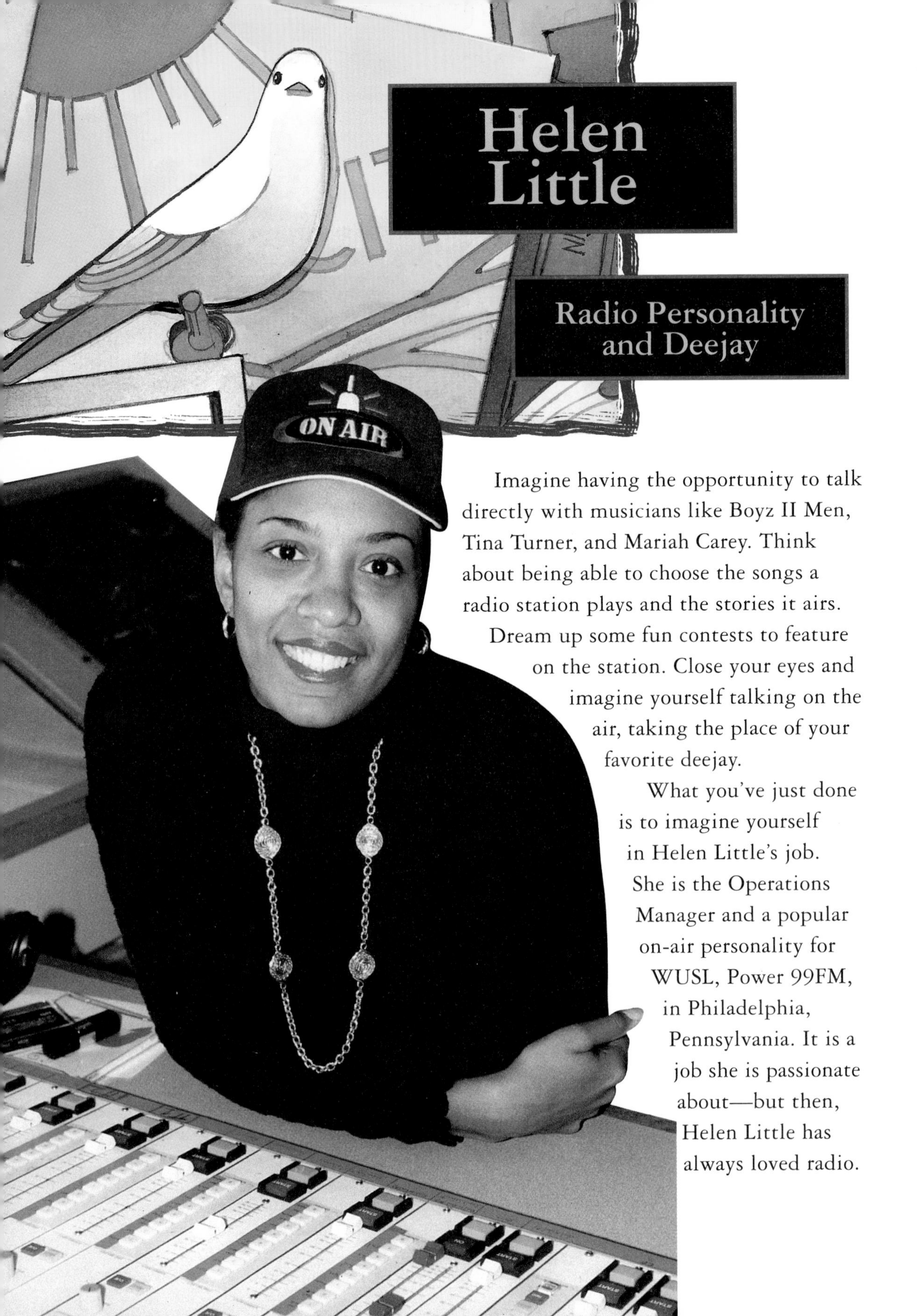

Helen Little

Radio Personality and Deejay

Imagine having the opportunity to talk directly with musicians like Boyz II Men, Tina Turner, and Mariah Carey. Think about being able to choose the songs a radio station plays and the stories it airs. Dream up some fun contests to feature on the station. Close your eyes and imagine yourself talking on the air, taking the place of your favorite deejay.

What you've just done is to imagine yourself in Helen Little's job. She is the Operations Manager and a popular on-air personality for WUSL, Power 99FM, in Philadelphia, Pennsylvania. It is a job she is passionate about—but then, Helen Little has always loved radio.

At a young age, Helen decided she wanted to be on the radio. She wanted to be a singer. She spent all her free time listening to the radio:

> "After dinner and homework, while the rest of my family was watching TV together, I was listening to the radio. So I got to know it from the outside looking in first."

Later, after high school, Helen shifted her goal to becoming a deejay. She wanted to communicate with others, and radio was perfect: "Since I was shy it worked for me because I didn't see the people I talked to."

In college at the University of North Carolina at Chapel Hill, Helen continued to nurture her dream of becoming a deejay. She took courses. She got a part-time radio job, talked to lots of people, and attended conferences and **seminars** (advanced courses students take in groups). All the while, Helen continued to listen to radio every possible minute.

By 1982, Little had fulfilled her dream. She was a radio deejay! Fourteen years later she is now the only African American female in the country named Operations Manager at an FM station.

"Dream BIG! You really can be whatever you want."

Helen Little encourages students like you to follow your dreams, too: "Dream BIG! You really can be whatever you want. Just don't give up! But as you climb the ladder of success be mindful of others and how you carry yourself. The people you see on the way up to the top are the same ones you'll see on the way down."

In keeping with these statements, Helen chooses Trustworthiness and Responsibility as the most important *Pillars of Character*: "Truth and sincerity as well as keeping commitments, mainly my commitments to myself, coupled with doing my best and never giving up are why I continue to grow."

Helen Little's success has come from commitment and hard work. It pays off the most, she says, "when the music and information that my station gives over the air make someone's day brighter."

Critical Thinking

1. What led Helen to choose a career in radio?
2. How did Helen prepare for her career?
3. How would you describe Helen Little's character?
4. What is Little's goal on a daily basis?

Trustworthiness

Responsibility

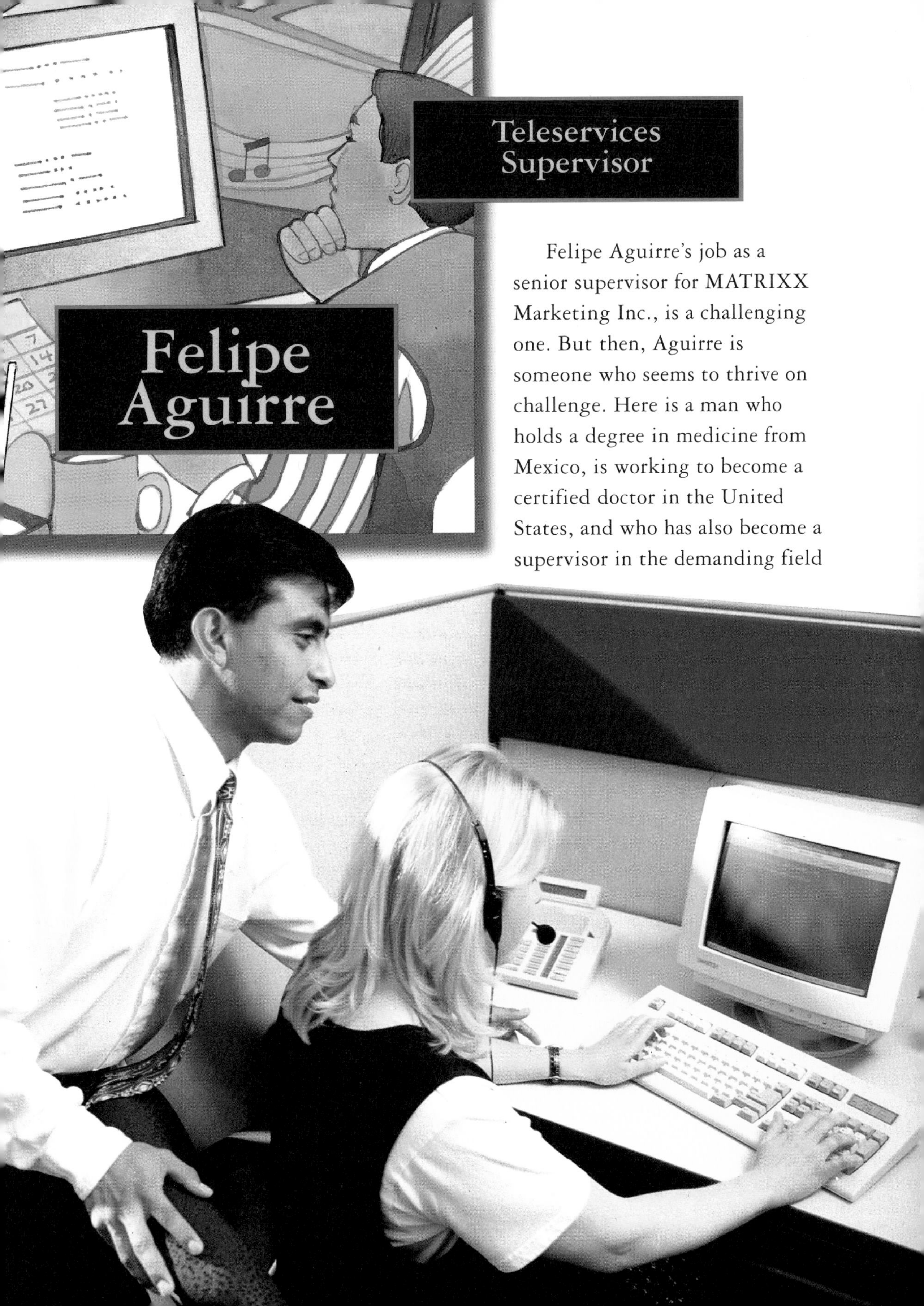

Felipe Aguirre

Teleservices Supervisor

Felipe Aguirre's job as a senior supervisor for MATRIXX Marketing Inc., is a challenging one. But then, Aguirre is someone who seems to thrive on challenge. Here is a man who holds a degree in medicine from Mexico, is working to become a certified doctor in the United States, and who has also become a supervisor in the demanding field

“This field requires self-direction and creativity.”

of telephone customer service. (In this position, he works on a medical-related account—combining his knowledge of medicine and his skills in customer service.) Even more astonishing is the fact that Felipe Aguirre has not yet celebrated his 30th birthday!

What powers Aguirre toward his success? The answer is found in his personality. As he says regarding his job at MATRIXX:

> “My career demands excellent communication and voice skills. Individuals who love challenge, who take initiative and make things happen, will succeed. This field requires self-direction and creativity. It demands leaders. I meet the criteria.”

Aguirre has learned the special skills used in telephone customer service and in management by taking courses on these topics. He believes in learning as much as possible, and he is intense about his studies. As he comments, “The most effective way for me to learn is to really remain focused while being instructed in the classroom. It makes things a lot easier while doing homework or reviewing information for an upcoming test!"

Aguirre also depends on his own good character to experience success as a supervisor. He is especially committed to the character trait Fairness. In a field that depends on using words well, being fair when communicating is a must. Felipe explains:

> "Listening to people's concerns and acting upon them in a timely manner builds loyalty and accountability on my part. Trust from my co-workers and clients is the natural end result."

Obviously, teleservice representatives today require much more than the "gift of gab." They need education, commitment, and good character. . . criteria which Felipe Aguirre has. He also has something else, a positive **attitude**, which he encourages you to acquire: "ALWAYS keep in mind that your potential, whether high or low, is determined by your own state of mind."

"Your potential...is determined by your own state of mind."

Critical Thinking

1. In addition to teleservices, what is Felipe's other career interest?
2. What skills are required in teleservices?
3. How has Felipe learned the skills for telephone customer service and management?
4. How would you describe Felipe Aguirre's character?

Fairness

Ann Symons

Librarian

Ann Symons beautifully sums up the job of a librarian in one sentence: "Librarianship is bringing people and information together." What this means for Symons is that she is able to enjoy her job nearly all the time. You see, Symons loves to work with people, *and* she loves to work with information—written, spoken, and technology-generated. In fact, the only time Symons feels frustrated with her work is when she doesn't have enough information available to meet the needs of the people using her library.

The people Symons serves as librarian are the students and staff at Juneau-Douglas High School in Juneau, Alaska. Working with this group is especially exciting, she says, because her work becomes part of the learning process. She is "busy every minute," pushing to provide diverse and up-to-date resources on the wide range of topics requested. She feels pleased and successful when she sees students working, thinking, coming up with new ideas or conclusions of their own, using information they have found.

Symons is particularly passionate about providing students with **intellectual freedom**, or the right of every person to have access to information. She has gained much recognition nationwide for her efforts in this area. For example, in 1996 she won the American Association of School Librarians (AASL) Intellectual Freedom Award. Symons is very active in the American Library Association. She says that this involvement "adds a dimension to my work that keeps me fresh, always looking for ways to promote libraries."

Even though Symons has been a librarian for more than 25 years, she certainly has had no problem remaining "fresh." She's on top of technology and pleased about how it can help librarians with their mission: "to connect people with the information they need to live, learn, and work in a democratic society."

Symons, like many librarians, didn't prepare for her career until after completing college. While working as a clerk at a hospital, she decided she wanted to be a librarian. She then went back to school and earned a masters degree in library science. She has been happily working in the field ever since. Her lifelong love for reading has certainly been well served by this career.

Symons finds it hard to choose one *Pillar of Character* as most important to her, but she does narrow the list to three: Respect for Others, Trustworthiness,

"Librarianship is bringing people and information together."

and Fairness. As she explains:

"In my job I work very hard to make sure that each person who comes to use the library is treated with respect, no matter what their question or need for information. Kids and teachers have to trust that you will meet their needs and that your fairness means everyone gets help."

Symons has practical advice for students like you. She encourages you to volunteer in your community as a way of gaining work experience. She feels that when you volunteer, you can find out what sort of work you can do to make a difference. We all make a difference in one way or another. For Ann Symons, this is the reward of being a librarian.

"I work very hard to make sure that each person who comes to use the library is treated with respect."

Respect for Others

Trustworthiness

Fairness

Critical Thinking

1. How does Ann Symons define her work as a librarian?
2. In what ways does Ann add extra dimensions to her work in the Juneau-Douglas High School library?
3. How did Ann become a librarian?
4. How would you describe Ann Symons's character?

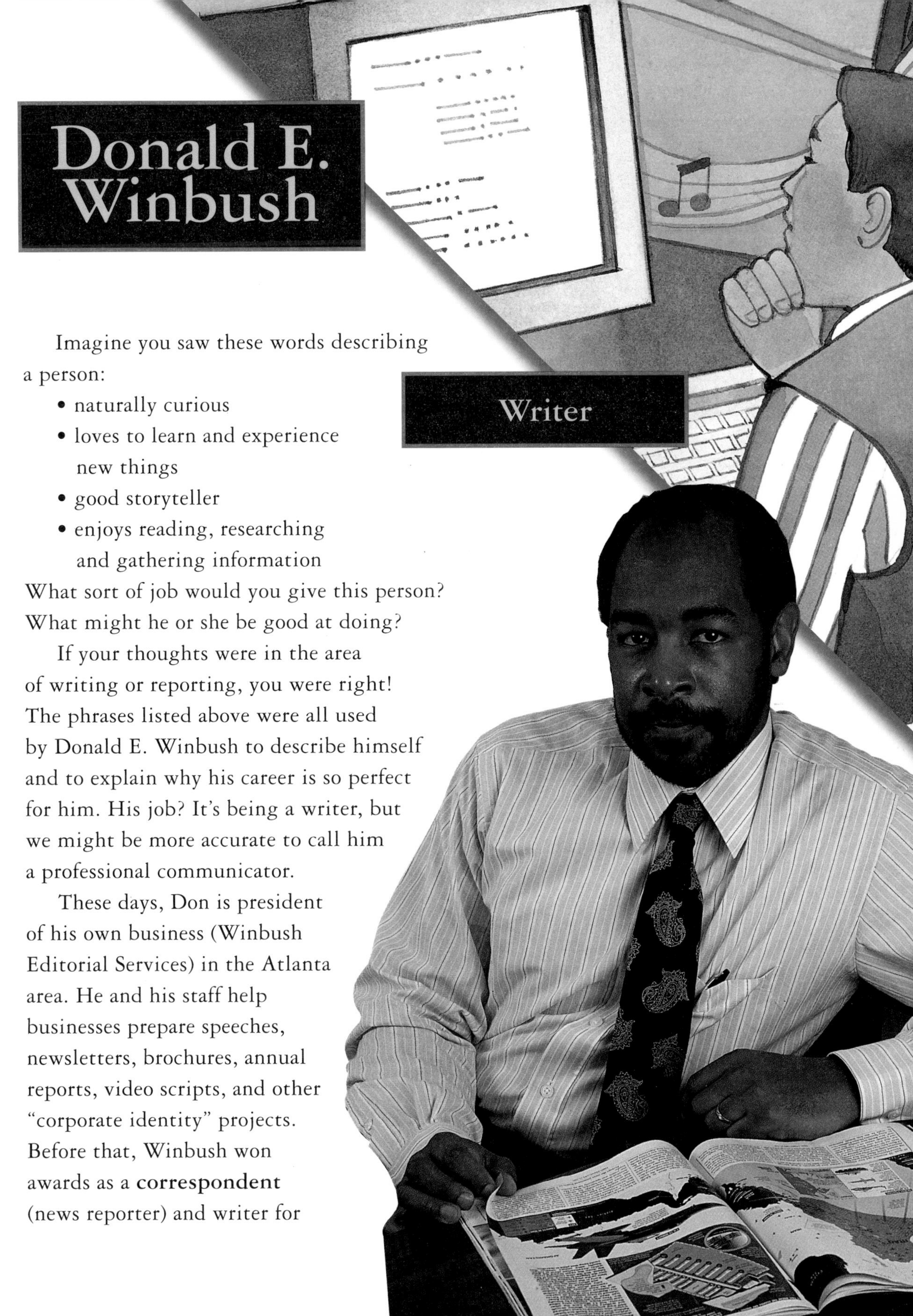

Donald E. Winbush

Writer

Imagine you saw these words describing a person:

- naturally curious
- loves to learn and experience new things
- good storyteller
- enjoys reading, researching and gathering information

What sort of job would you give this person? What might he or she be good at doing?

If your thoughts were in the area of writing or reporting, you were right! The phrases listed above were all used by Donald E. Winbush to describe himself and to explain why his career is so perfect for him. His job? It's being a writer, but we might be more accurate to call him a professional communicator.

These days, Don is president of his own business (Winbush Editorial Services) in the Atlanta area. He and his staff help businesses prepare speeches, newsletters, brochures, annual reports, video scripts, and other "corporate identity" projects. Before that, Winbush won awards as a **correspondent** (news reporter) and writer for

TIME magazine. In the span of his 25-year career, he also has taught on the college level, been a radio show host, and written for newspapers. As you can see, he has communicated professionally through most media!

Winbush became interested in the field of **journalism** (the work of gathering and preparing news) when he was in tenth grade in Winona, Mississippi. During a "career day" program at the weekly school assembly, Don focused on a classmate's report regarding journalism. As he says:

> "Being a journalist seemed fascinating—that today would be different from the day before. It sounded thrilling—anything but boring and routine. It promised a sense of adventure that turned me on."

Winbush did not wait to get involved in journalism. He began writing a regular piece for the school newspaper. His topic was something like "what's happening on campus." He gave his reporting a unique twist, however:

> "I tried to spice it up by using phrases and titles of popular songs—which gave the stories a certain flavor that seemed to catch people's fancy."

The praise and success he experienced boosted Don's confidence and set him on a sure course toward "creatively writing things for public consumption."

"Character takes courage. Always try."

After high school, Don earned a degree in communications from the University of Memphis. He has enjoyed his career ever since. One thing he especially likes is the later stages of the writing process. He calls it "the polishing, polishing, and re-polishing that takes place toward the end." This fits in with Don Winbush's acute sense of Responsibility when it comes to his daily work. He understands well the power and influence of the media and works hard never to misrepresent information.

It's accurate to say that Don Winbush uses his talents as a writer in uplifting ways. He seeks to inspire and benefit others. He understands the permanence of the written word, and he has the courage to write with character. He encourages students like you to live with character and to always keep trying.

Critical Thinking

1. How did Donald become interested in journalism?
2. What was the creative twist in Donald's first work as a writer?
3. How did Winbush prepare for his career?
4. How would you describe Donald Winbush's character?

Responsibility

Group Project

Designing Greeting Cards

Work with a group of four or five students to design a set of greeting cards. One purpose of this project is to work with words, so you can be as creative as possible. As you work, pay attention to how you feel about working with words. What about it feels natural? Another purpose of this project is to come up with greeting cards that are relevant to your lives now. Celebrate small successes. Console a disappointed friend. You might choose to have humorous cards, serious cards, food and animal cards...anything but wordless cards.

Remember to use your best character traits as you work with your group.

Materials — heavy paper or card stock, colored pens and pencils, calligraphy markers, pencils and erasers, magazine pictures, glue, scissors

Method — Brainstorm together the kind of look you want for your line of cards. Or perhaps you will choose to have a combination of styles. Then list the occasions that warrant one of your fine greeting cards. As a group, write the verses (which may or may not rhyme) for each of your cards. You might do this as a progressive story, where each one of you contributes a line, one or more times until the text is complete. Decide on the kind of art for your cards. You might draw illustrations or use pictures from magazines. Take care over hand-lettering the cards. Alternatively, you might wish to use a computer. Use a great typeface, cut out the text, and glue it into your cards.

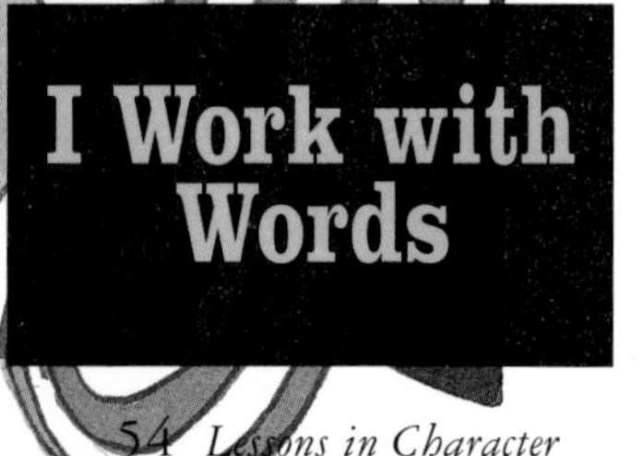

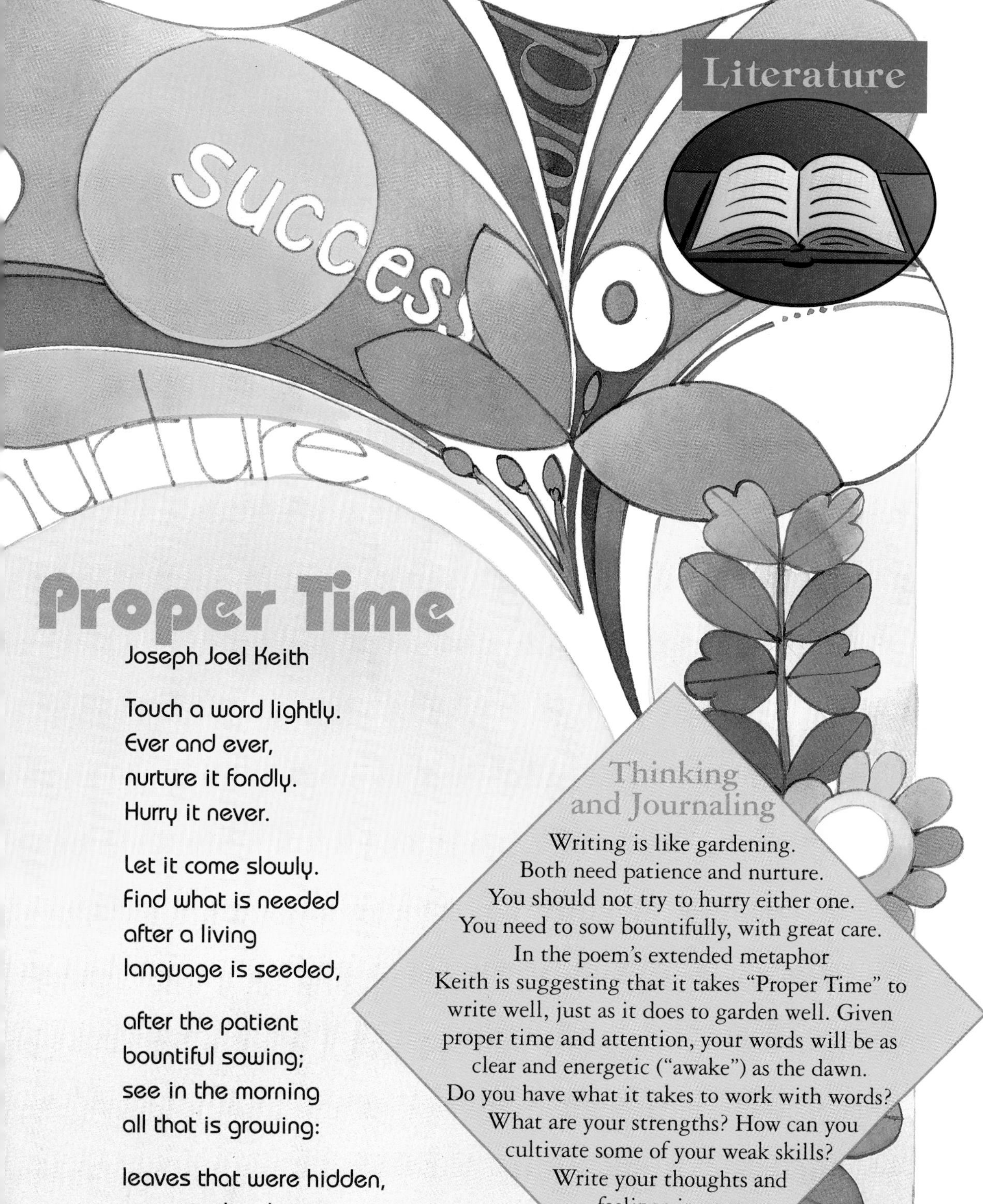

Proper Time

Joseph Joel Keith

Touch a word lightly.
Ever and ever,
nurture it fondly.
Hurry it never.

Let it come slowly.
Find what is needed
after a living
language is seeded,

after the patient
bountiful sowing;
see in the morning
all that is growing:

leaves that were hidden,
green in the shower;
words as awake as
the crowing hour.

Thinking and Journaling

Writing is like gardening. Both need patience and nurture. You should not try to hurry either one. You need to sow bountifully, with great care. In the poem's extended metaphor Keith is suggesting that it takes "Proper Time" to write well, just as it does to garden well. Given proper time and attention, your words will be as clear and energetic ("awake") as the dawn. Do you have what it takes to work with words? What are your strengths? How can you cultivate some of your weak skills? Write your thoughts and feelings in your journal.

Writing

Poetry

Description Poetry comes in many shapes and sizes, from silly limericks to solemn odes. A good poem surprises you in some way; it helps you take a new look at something familiar. Poetry depends on sounds, whether rhyme is used or not. It almost always has rhythm, which may come in part from repetition. Most poetry is condensed, concentrated, and intense. Like song lyrics, poems can evoke powerful feelings ranging from joy to grief to rage.

A poem reflects something the poet cares about. Poems usually:

- Play with sounds.
- Repeat words, phrases, or lines.
- Show something in a new way, whether it be comical or serious.

Assignment Think of a time when using words did not work out for you, or a time when using words worked out especially well. Maybe you meant to say one thing and exactly the opposite came out. Perhaps you said what you meant, but your listener heard something entirely different. Or maybe you gave the perfect response to a question.

Your poem will be stronger if you work from real life, but you may combine details from different times. Using the steps in the writing process, write a poem about your miscommunication or great communication. If you get stuck, you could repeat the following starters to begin your lines.

I meant to say. . .

But she/he heard. . .

PREWRITING DRAFTING REVISING PROOFREADING PUBLISHING

Purposes to entertain, to express feelings

Audience your classmates, or children

My Work as a Student

Pair Share

Careers — Work with a partner. Each of you will choose one of the people in this unit. Review the work that each person does. Then compare their work. In what ways is it similar? In what ways is it different? (Think about training, practice, place of work, and so on.)

What are you learning at school that would help you prepare for similar careers?

Character — *Trustworthiness* is one of the character traits Helen Little finds important in her work in radio. In what ways can you relate trustworthiness to your work at school? (You might think about ways other people depend on you and about times when you give your word.) List the many ways you are trustworthy in your life at school.

How can you tell when you are being trustworthy? What feelings do you feel? What thoughts do you think?

Set a goal of a new way you want to be trustworthy at school in the near future.

Trustworthiness

I Work Outside

UNIT FOUR

Beauty *by E-Yeh-Shure*

Beauty is seen
In the sunlight,
The trees, the birds,
Corn growing and people working
Or dancing for their harvest.

Beauty is heard
In the night,
Wind sighing, rain falling,
Or a singer chanting
Anything in earnest.

Beauty is in yourself.
Good deeds, happy thoughts
That repeat themselves
In your dreams,
In your work,
And even in your rest.

The Native American woman who wrote this poem loved the beauty of the outdoors. By seeing, hearing, and feeling the natural world, she gained happiness and goodness.

You might know someone like this poet, a person whom you can't imagine being "cooped up" inside day after day. You yourself might be this type of person. Fortunately, there are many jobs that allow workers to be outside, to experience nature every day.

In this unit you will read about four careers in which the work takes place outdoors. You will meet four people of character who, like E-Yeh-Shure, find "good deeds, happy thoughts" because of their ability to earn a living while enjoying nature's beauty.

Thomas Barth

Crane Operator

In the community of crane operators, Thomas Barth is among the elite. He is one of about 120 people in the United States who have received certification to inspect cranes. The importance of this job becomes clear when you think of what could happen if a crane **malfunctioned.** Imagine if a 100-ton load was dropped, or a crane's boon suddenly slammed into a building! The results of such an accident would be horrible. That, says Thomas Barth, is why crane operators, inspectors, and instructors must take their responsibilities so seriously.

> "Responsibility is the most important *Pillar of Character* in my work because accidents can occur quickly. . . . You can't let anyone push you into doing something that might be dangerous or unsafe."

For 30 years, Thomas Barth has been responsibly operating cranes. To put it simply, he loves his job. As he says, "I live, eat, and exist because of cranes." He's felt this way since junior high school when he saw a crane up close for the first time. From his seat in the classroom, he had a view of a crane at work on the school grounds. He could tell how important the crane operator was to the success of the project: "Everyone from the job superintendent to the laborers were talking to the crane operator. That's when I decided I wanted to do that."

Barth has earned his great reputation in the prestigious world of crane operators by being a good, dependable worker. He's benefitted from on-the-job training and specialty schools, some of which are run by crane manufacturers. But mostly Barth believes it's his own hard work that helped him get ahead. What other personal qualities have helped with his particular job? Barth lists several: patience, good coordination, alertness, ability to see all the details within the "big picture," and careful decision-making.

"You can't let anyone push you into doing something that might be dangerous or unsafe."

In the end, though, Barth will always bring it back to hard work. That's why, in Alaska, where Barth lives and works, you can find him taking advantage of the days when the sun never sets. If you see a crane against the bright midnight sky on these nights, there's a good chance Thomas Barth is in the cab, deftly moving tons of materials. . . and smiling.

> "I live, eat, and exist because of cranes."

Critical Thinking

1. How did Thomas become interested in being a crane operator?
2. What is the most important thing that has helped Thomas get ahead in his job?
3. What else has helped Barth succeed in his work as a crane operator?
4. How would you describe Thomas Barth's character?

Responsibility

Zoo Curator

Lorraine Smith

The interests that led Lorraine Smith to her career coincided nicely with what was happening in zoos in the late 1970s. As a college student at Michigan State University, Lorraine became very interested in the **conservation** of endangered animals. She decided she wanted to make a personal contribution to efforts to save animals. As she looked into the issue, she found that zoos were becoming more and more involved in conservation and education. Working in a zoo, she decided, would allow her to join the conservation community. Lorraine therefore got her degree in **zoology** (the study of animal life) and has worked full-time in zoos since 1983.

"I don't mind getting dirty and working hard."

Today, at the North Carolina Zoological Park in Asheboro, Smith is the **Curator** of Mammals. This means she is in charge of caring for animals such as bears, cats (lions, cougars, bobcats, etc.), seals, monkeys, giraffes, zebra, bats, and rodents. She is very happy with her job, finding it both challenging and rewarding. She enjoys the fact that she is continuously learning (she reads all she can about animals in her care), but she also enjoys the day-to-day functions of her work. As she comments: "My career appeals to me on a very academic level and also at a more basic level. I love to be outside; I don't mind getting dirty and working hard. A career with animals often involves unusual and sometimes very long work hours. But the rewards are there for those who truly enjoy the challenges and experiences."

Smith also appreciates the opportunity to travel that her job provides. She has visited Indonesia and Africa, for example, and thoroughly enjoyed exploring the unique aspects of these distant countries.

The challenge that perhaps forms the core of Smith's work is defined by her as follows.

> "In zoos we are challenged to provide the animals with the opportunity to express their natural behaviors. It is important for the visitors to see animals behaving much as they do in the wild; this helps them to gain an understanding of that species and why we should conserve it in its natural home."

Environmental enrichment is the process Smith and other zookeepers use to encourage animals' natural behaviors. Things like food, proper living areas and conditions, and the presence of authentic trees and bushes are all carefully considered as zookeepers strive to mimic "life in the wild" for the animals in their charge.

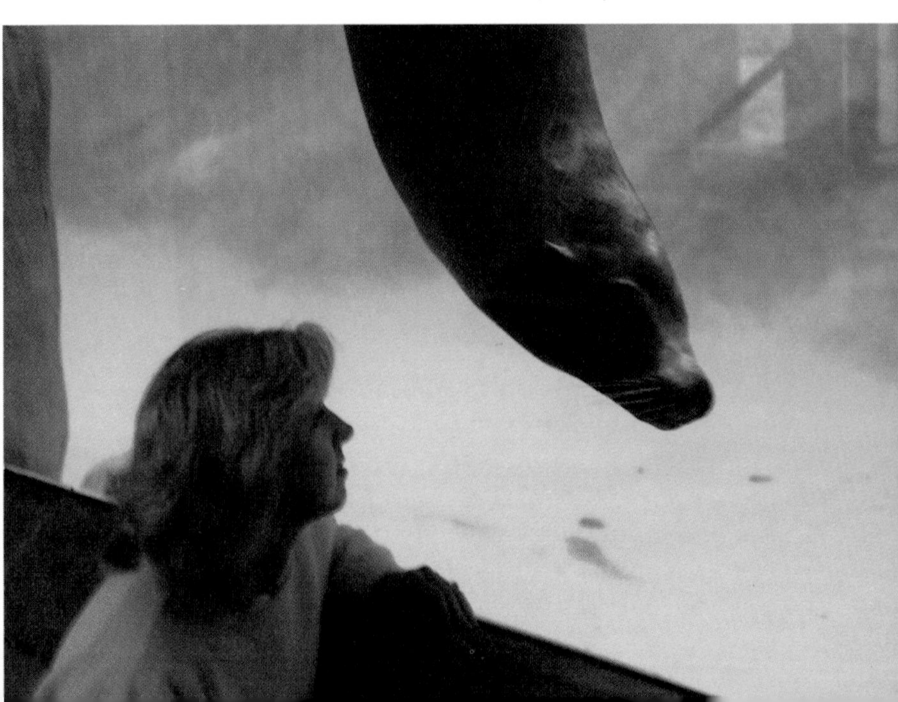

Success in her work and in the efforts of the whole conservation movement depends, Smith believes, on the character trait Citizenship. The importance of community is key. As she says:

> "We are part of so many communities: local, regional, and global. Everyone can make a difference in his or her small part of the world. . . working within a community helps you to accomplish your goals."

Smith also suggests that students your age can begin now to pursue your interests. "Don't give up. Read and try to learn more about the things you find most interesting in this world." Lorraine Smith is living proof that interests and work can be a perfect match.

"Working within a community helps you to accomplish your goals."

CITIZENSHIP

Critical Thinking

1. How did Lorraine choose her career?
2. What are two different levels of Lorraine's work as Curator of Mammals?
3. Why does Smith strive to provide a natural, authentic environment for the animals?
4. How would you describe Lorraine Smith's character?

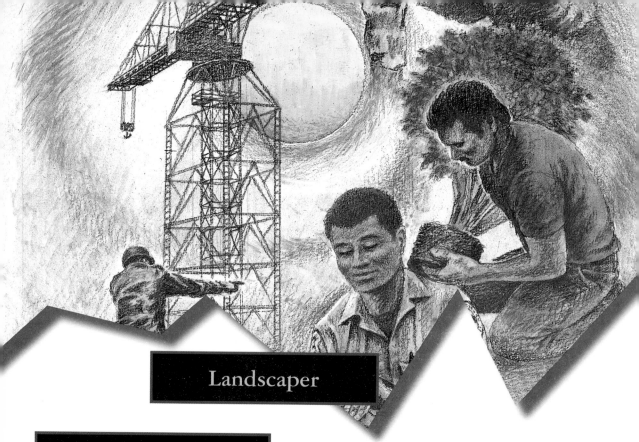

Landscaper

Walter Imahara

Walter Imahara is a decision-maker, and many people in Baton Rouge are happy about that. You see, often when Imahara makes a decision, beauty is the result. That's because he owns a landscape company. His decisions result in beautiful, award-winning lawns and gardens throughout his area of Louisiana.

Making decisions and following through on them seems to have always come easily to Imahara. When he was only 18 years old, he decided to enter the field of **horticulture.** He chose to study this science of how to grow flowers, shrubs, vegetables, and fruits at the University of Southwestern Louisiana (USL). He received his degree in 1960. He then served as an officer in the United States Army. Nevertheless, his long and notable career as a nurseryman was already taking root.

Another important part of Imahara's life also began while he was at USL: weightlifting. His decision to participate in this sport was typically fruitful for him. He was the first person at USL to earn a letter in the sport. While there, he won three national collegiate meets. Like his landscaping, however, Imahara's weightlifting was just beginning when he left college. Today he is a World Masters Chairman in the sport, competing at the Masters level. In 1996, for example, he won the Gold Medal for his class at the National Master, ProAm Master, and World Masters championships.

> "Trustworthiness is the foundation on which character should be built."

Part of Imahara's ability to focus on and reach his goals surely comes from his upbringing. As he says, "My parents were emphatic about my receiving an education and being self-reliant. They said, 'Be your own boss.'" Imahara agrees with this advice and encourages young people today to focus on getting a college education in a "sellable" field.

Imahara also acknowledges the special importance to him of two *Pillars of Character:* Trustworthiness and Respect for Others. He labels Trustworthiness as "the foundation on which character should be built." Daily, he shows others respect, and he hopes to receive their respect in return.

Given all of Imahara's accomplishments, it's certainly no surprise that December 9, 1992, was proclaimed "Walter M. Imahara Day" by the mayor of Baton Rouge. In fact, you could say that was one wise decision.

Trustworthiness

Respect for Others

Critical Thinking

1. What is the result of Walter Imahara's decision making as a landscaper?
2. What professional training helped Walter prepare for his career?
3. When Imahara studied horticulture, what did he learn?
4. How would you describe Walter Imahara's character?

Mitchell Marken, Ph.D.

Archaeologist

Mitch Marken describes the job of an **archaeologist** very well:

> "Archaeologists study the remains left by people in the past. We study these things (called **artifacts**) to get a better idea of how people lived, and why they did the things they did in history. We work outside (we call it 'in the field') and inside ('in the lab') where we write about the things we find, draw the artifacts and study them."

Isn't that a clear explanation? Marken has been an archaeologist for about 14 years, so you can be sure he really knows (and loves!) his job.

Mitch Marken first became committed to archaeology as a career shortly after graduating from high school in Santa Cruz, California. He went on an expedition to Greece as a volunteer for an archaeological project. . . and he knew

this work was for him. However, his interest in "going to look for stuff" has always been with him. Also, he remembers a biology teacher in junior high school whose words about science seem especially relevant to the field of archaeology:

> "The great thing about science is that we get to stand on the shoulders of all those that have gone before us, without having to start on our own."

Once Mitch became committed to this career, he went to college in San Francisco. After working for a few years, he decided to pursue a graduate degree. He found a program that matched his special interests. It was at the University of St. Andrews in Scotland, and the program was Maritime Archaeology (the history of people and the sea). In 1991, Marken received his doctorate (the "Ph.D." after his name) in this field.

"Learn as much as you can, every day you can."

Today Marken works at Summit Envirosolutions in Reno, Nevada. He is now a senior archaeologist, but his love for his job is as fresh as ever. He comments:

> "First and foremost, there is the excitement of discovering new things, and visiting new places for work. I like to do many different things instead of the same thing over and over again. I get to go into the field, walk outside, dive on shipwrecks, dig holes, draw pictures, make maps, take photographs, use computers, do research in libraries and write reports. . ."

With this many different jobs and skills in his life, it's no surprise that Mitch urges students like you to remember the richness of life: "Learn as much as you can, every day you can. Everything you are now learning has a place in whatever you will do in life."

Some things *do* remain constant in Marken's work. One is his commitment to all six *Pillars of Character*. Another is his daily use of a decision-making model like STAR. His work, though exciting, requires careful planning. He must follow the steps in STAR to be successful. As he emphasizes, "You only have one chance to dig up a site without destroying the information."

Critical Thinking

1. Why did Mitch become interested in being an archaeologist?
2. What studies helped Marken prepare for his career?
3. How would you describe Mitchell Marken's character?
4. How might the steps of STAR help Mitch Marken be successful on an archaeological dig?

STAR

Group Project

Making a Mural

Work with a group of four or five students to make a mural. One purpose of this project is to experience working outside. So as you are working, examine your feelings and thoughts about outdoor work. As a group, come up with your idea of the absolute best work outside in the best place in the world. Maybe you are forest rangers or life guards or something more unusual and surprising. Include yourselves in the mural, hard at work outside in paradise. Remember to use your best character traits as you work with your group.

Materials — long sheets of butcher paper, masking tape, tempera paints and brushes, colored markers, construction paper, scissors, glue, foil

Method — You might want to use pencil to outline your basic plan. Use your butcher paper on a sidewalk or other flat surface outdoors. Decide on a location to make your mural, and tape your long piece of butcher paper up. This could be on the side of a building, around a huge tree, against a fence, etc. Use a variety of media and methods to create your mural. One fun addition is to make speech balloons with comments about your outdoor work in paradise.

I Work Outside

Literature

The Performers

Robert Hayden

Easily, almost matter-of-factly they step,
two minor Wallendas, with pail and
squeegee along
the wintry ledge, hook their harness to the wall
and leaning back into a seven-story angle of space
begin washing the office windows. I
am up there too until straps break
and iron paper apple of iron I fall
through plateglass wind onto stalagmites below.

But am safely at my desk again by the time
the hairline walkers, high-edge
balancers end their center-ring routine
and crawl inside. A rough day, I remark,
for such a risky business. Many thanks.
Thank you, sir, one of the men replies.

Thinking and Journaling

This poet gives a powerful picture of the window washers, two minor Wallendas, famous high-wire circus performers. Doesn't the "angle of space" help you feel what it's like to hang there over nothing but air? From inside his office, the poet fantasizes himself outside, himself doing this risky business, daring fate, working in the cold. Suddenly he pictures himself falling seven stories onto objects on the sidewalk below.

Later, his fantasy over, the workday over, the office worker thanks the window washers. What do you think he might be thanking them for? What would be great about doing this daring outdoor work? Which of these two kinds of work would be more natural for you? Why do you think so? Write your thoughts and feelings in your journal.

Writing

Adventure Fiction

Description A good rollicking adventure story gets your pulse racing and your eyes flying across the page. It transports you to the deck of the sailboat in the storm, to the tree top in the raging wind where your pet cat is stranded. Often you find yourself in a struggle against nature or fate—with only your quick wit, imagination, and muscles to see you through.

As with other fiction, adventure stories include a problem, the characters' attempts to solve it, and the resolution. Adventure stories often:

- Include some breathtaking action.
- Give special attention to the physical details of the setting.
- Show the stress the characters are feeling.

Assignment Picture yourself in some thrilling outdoor work. What is the wildest adventure that might threaten you? Is nature your foe? Are there wild beasts? Or is the problem that your locomotive engine has gone out of control on the longest downhill stretch? Remember, in fiction you may have superhuman prowess and brilliance. Using the writing process, write a story about your imagined adventure. Let your reader get caught up in it with you. And then bring us safely home.

PREWRITING DRAFTING REVISING PROOFREADING PUBLISHING

Purpose to describe a fictional event

Audience your classmates

My Work as a Student

Pair Share

Careers — Work with a partner. Each of you will choose one of the people in this unit. Review the work that each person does. Then compare their work. In what ways is it similar? In what ways is it different? (Think about training, practice, place of work, and so on.)

What are you learning at school that would help you prepare for similar careers?

Character — Mitch Marken stresses STAR as an important foundation for his work in archaeology. In what ways do you use STAR in your work at school? (You might consider each step of STAR as well as the whole process.) List the many times using STAR makes a difference for you.

How can you tell when you are using STAR effectively? What feelings do you feel? What thoughts do you think? Set a goal of a new way you want to use STAR at school in the near future.

I Work in an Office

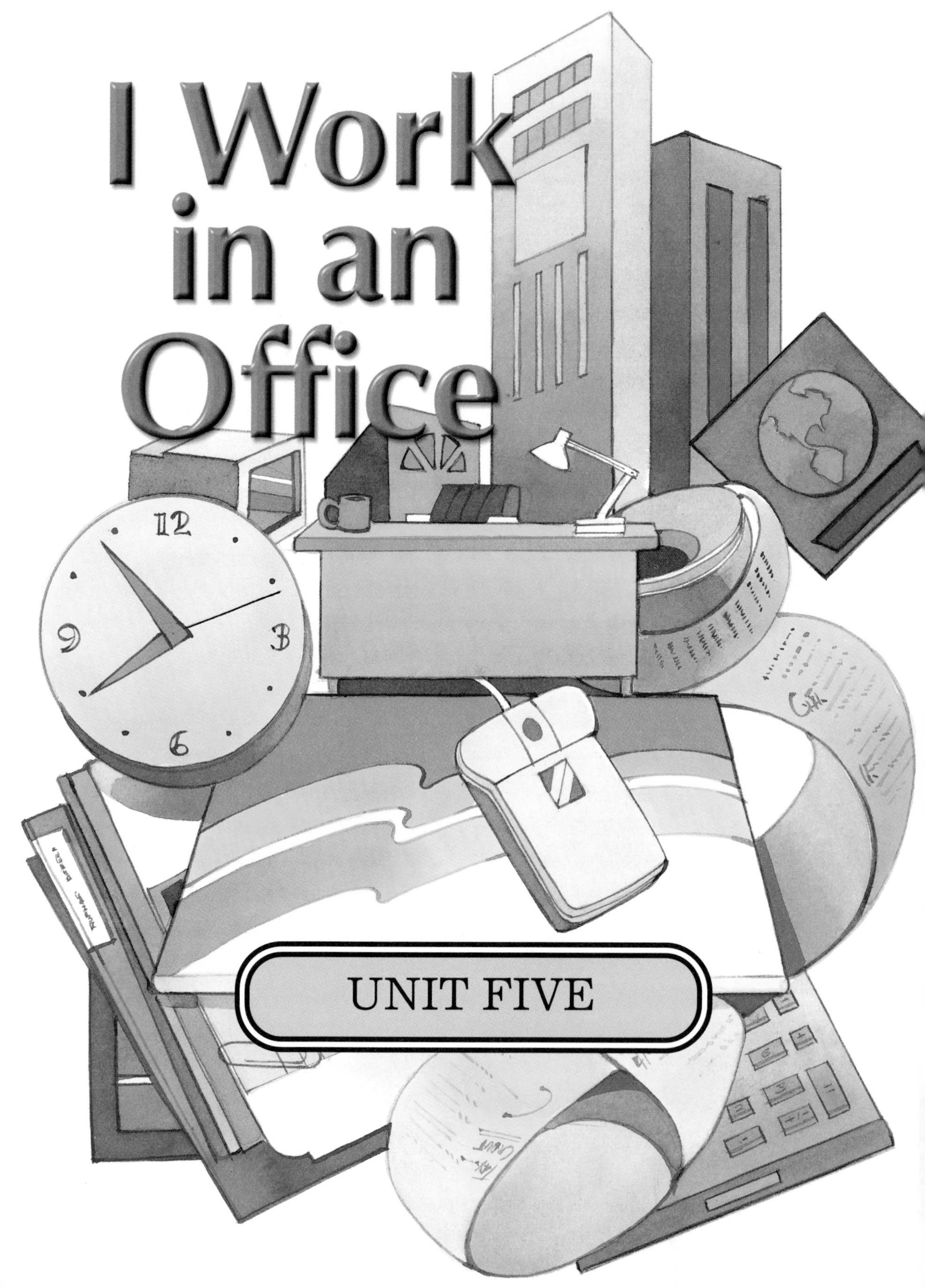

UNIT FIVE

On this page and the next are two poems about life in the office. Read to find out what working in an office can be like. Would you like it?

Ms

by Judith Berke

This desk is an antique: it's dainty,
and has limbs, and boy are they shaky.
My boss is a woman, and luckily,
she got this really nifty desk for her office,
maybe to make up for something.
Today when I brought in coffee,
Mr. Tull was in the small chair, and
Mr. Royce on the desk, and then
Mr. Chagrew on the windowsill, you
know, like steps, so the big
boss just stood there and loomed
over them. I brought the messages in,
all folded up, like she likes them. The one I
wrote said: Maybe we should put a chair up
on the ceiling? That she kept stabbing at
like a shish kebab, maybe to keep
from laughing. Then she said, Violet,
get a more comfortable chair for Mr. Ruby
(he's the president), so I knew then
we had to put them in just
the right order, sort of like checkers
or musical chairs; and that's the way it is
here—everyone moves one over. Once I said
to my boss, Did you ever see the TV show
about the baboons? Actually my boss looks
like Jane Goodall—you know, delicate, except
of course she's part of the tribe now.
That's why she wears the jacket
with the shoulders. Sometimes we eat lunch
here in her office, and there she is,
her head back in the chair, swiveling,
and the jacket, like another person,
in back of her.

The Man in the Open Doorway

by Dana Gioia

This is the world in which he lives:
Four walls, a desk, a swivel chair,
A doorway with no door to close,
Vents to bring in air.

There are two well-marked calendars,
Some pencils, and a telephone
The women at the front desk answer
Leaving him alone.

There is a clock he hardly sees
Beside the window on the wall.
It moves in only one direction,
Never stops at all.

Outside the February wind
Scrapes up against the windowpane,
And a blue-green land is fading,
Scarred by streaks of rain.

The phones go off. The files are locked.
But the doorway still is lit at night
Like the tall window of a church
Bleached in winter light.

Sometimes the shadow of his hand
Falls from his desk onto the wall
And is the only thing that moves
Anywhere at all.

Or else he will drive back at night
To walk along the corridor
And, thinking of the day's success,
Trace his steps once more,

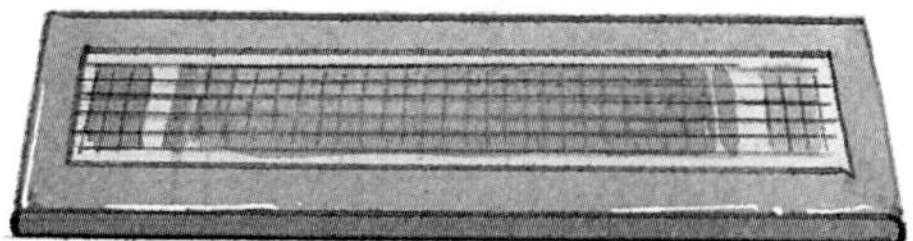

Then pause in a darkened stairway
Until the sounds of his steps
have ceased
And stroke the wall as if it were
Some attendant beast.

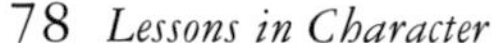

These two poets (both of whom, by the way, have experienced working in an office) have carefully described office details—furniture, equipment, and so on. This helps you imagine being in those offices. Through the language of the poems, you also get a feeling for how the workers in these offices view their work.

Both poets would surely agree that these offices are not perfect. However, the people who work in them truly enjoy it. Violet and her boss laugh together and respect each other. The man in the open doorway returns with pride to his office even at night. There seems to be something about the regularity of things in an office, the familiarity of daily work, that makes office workers happy.

Would you be happy working in an office? As you read this unit, you'll meet four people who are. As you learn about their jobs, you'll also see the importance of character in their lives and in their work.

Sanjay Jani

Architect

Growing up in India, Sanjay Jani had the opportunity to travel extensively with his family each year. He visited many beautiful places, both manmade and natural. As a child, he enjoyed the art present in these places. Whether he was looking at ancient temples, curving rivers, pottery, or city skylines, Sanjay had the ability to see and enjoy the beauty before him.

Today, as an **architect** (a person who designs buildings and other large

Patel residence

structures) in Iowa City, Iowa, Sanjay Jani is many miles away from his native Bombay, India. Yet the artistic sensitivity he showed as a child has never left him. By tenth grade he knew he wanted to be an architect. He concentrated on math, science, and drawing in high school, going on to earn college degrees in architecture. In this field Sanjay Jani has found the right combination of skills: "It includes drawing, dreaming, problem solving, art, and innovation. . . an enjoyable, fun profession."

"The process of listening, sketching, thinking, talking, improving, becomes art itself."

Jani's projects are mostly single-family homes. His clients, the people who hire him, benefit from his view of architecture as an art form. He describes his work: "Every client has similar requirements for a house but brings his or her own unique background, interests, and expectations from life. I try to interpret that poetically in the form of a house. The process of listening, sketching, thinking, talking, improving, becomes art itself."

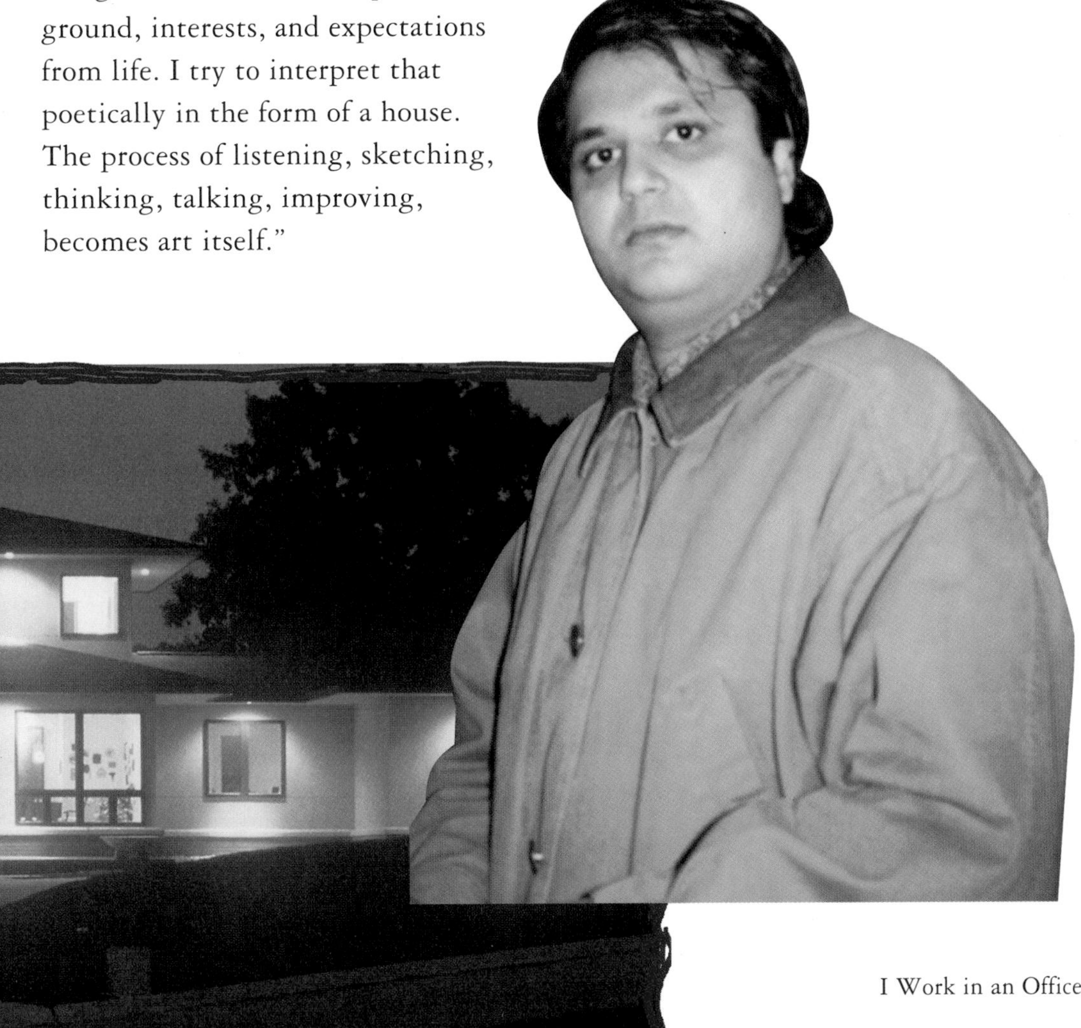

He particularly enjoys seeing a house finished, with his clients living in it happily.

If this career interests you, Jani suggests that you begin to look carefully at all objects around you—"from a coffee cup to a car to a building." As you begin to explore the art and the science behind objects, you will be taking on the curiosity of an architect.

Jani also stresses the importance of the pillar Responsibility in working as an architect. As he says, "My clients pay me a lot of money to design their dream house. I have to give my best in return." A look at some of his work is proof that Sanjay Jani does just that.

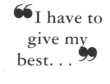

Patel residence

> "I have to give my best. . ."

Responsibility

Critical Thinking

1. In what ways did travel help Sanjay toward becoming an architect?
2. How did Sanjay's schooling help him prepare for his career?
3. How does Jani describe the combination of skills he uses in his work?
4. How would you describe Sanjay Jani's character?

Anne Frick

Travel Agent

When Anne Frick graduated from college in 1967, she intended to teach elementary school. But then her plans changed. She and her husband started a family, and she decided to stay home to do the important job of raising children.

As Anne's children reached school age, she began preparing herself to work outside the home. She went back to school, to Asheville-Buncombe Technical Institute in North Carolina. In 1977, she earned her degree in Secretarial Science and went to work.

Within three years, Frick had been named executive secretary to the vice president of a large company. Her skills, hard work, and helpful attitude were serving her well. But the opportunity to change her course came once again to Anne Frick.

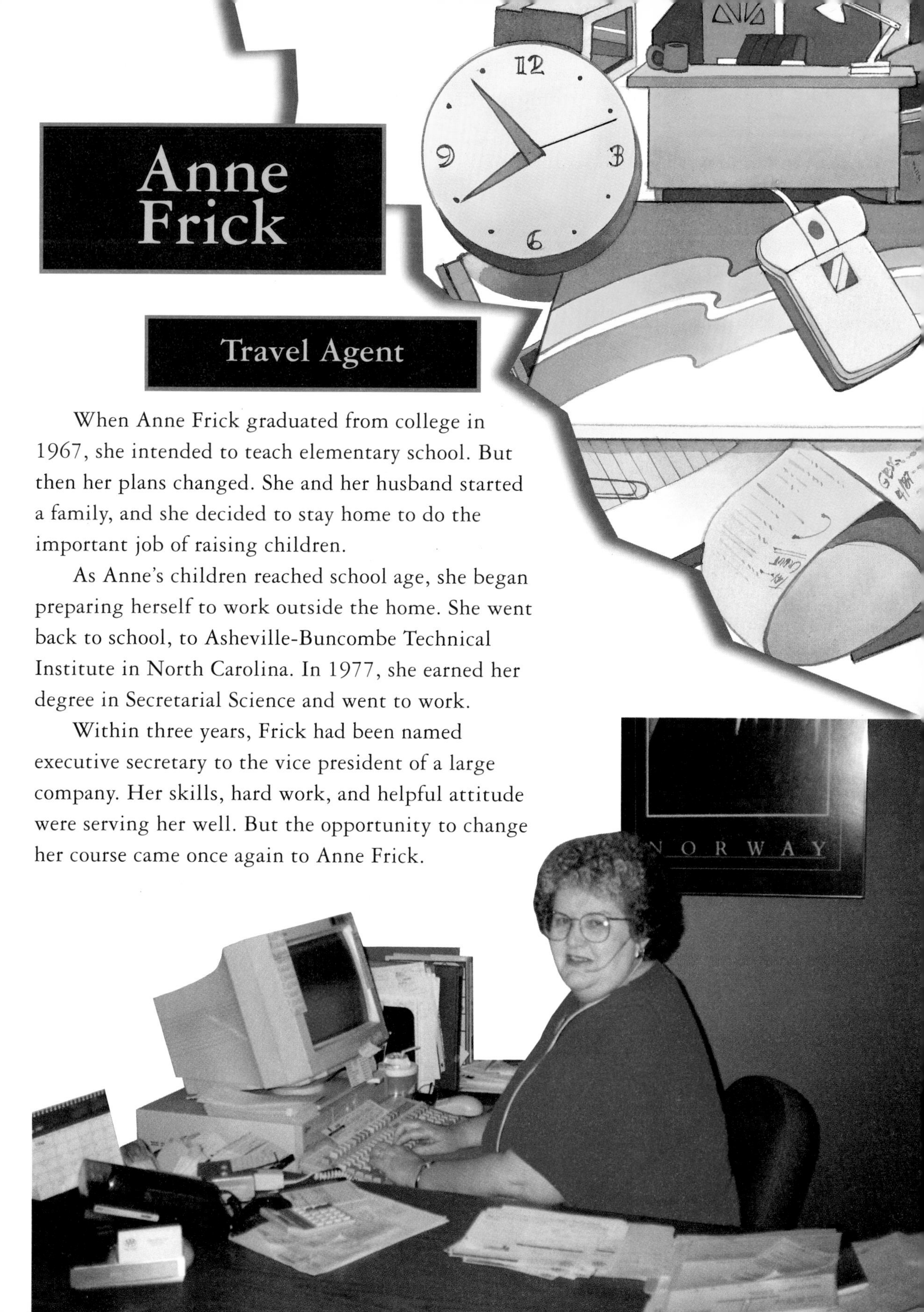

A friend of Anne had bought a travel agency, and he was having a hard time finding good employees. He offered Anne a job, and she took it. Once again, she adjusted beautifully to the change. As she explains: "The training I had as a secretary to a man who did a lot of traveling as well as the secretarial skills were helpful to me as a travel agent, but most of what I learned was on-the-job training."

Anne hastens to explain that today, agencies probably will not hire a person unless he or she attends a school with a specific travel agent training program. The ever-increasing role of computers in the travel industry is part of the reason why. As Frick says, "You can't quit learning." Over her 17 years in the field, Frick has worked hard to remain current. In 1986, for example, she received her Certified Travel Counselor designation. This means she completed a two-year, graduate level course in ethical and efficient travel agency management. It is a designation she received with pride. Daily, she feels proud and happy when a trip goes well for her clients. She enjoys hearing their reports—whether about a wonderful vacation or a hitch-free business trip.

Frick feels that Responsibility is the most important character trait for her. She believes in excellence at work, honesty, and **accountability** to her clients. If she needs to work early and late to handle a

"You can't quit learning."

rush situation, she does so. If she feels a trip wouldn't work well for a client, she says so. She pays attention to details, and she makes things happen smoothly.

Anne Frick offers advice to students like you that clearly comes from her own life experience: "Learn about different things so you can have options and choices. Being good at something doesn't necessarily mean that you like doing it. Don't be afraid to change careers if you find that what you are doing is not satisfying to you. Your interests may change as you grow older."

No doubt the clients of AAA Travel Agency in Asheville are hoping that Anne Frick's career changes are over.

Critical Thinking

1. What change in career plans did Anne make after graduating from college?
2. Describe the training Anne had in order to begin her career as a travel agent.
3. What continuing training has Frick had?
4. How would you describe Anne Frick's character?

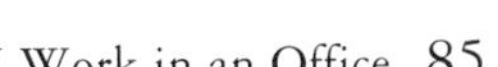

Marti Martin

Customer Service Representative

Marti Martin's official title at Peace Health, the clinic where she works in Florence, Oregon, is Customer Service Representative for the Billing Office. In this position Marti does much more than present patients with a bill. She helps them figure out how to pay it. As she says: "I like to think of myself as a patient advocate, rather than bill collector or secretary—and my job and skills lend well to this. It is possible to be both warm and caring and professional."

In fact, it was the supportive atmosphere of the clinic offices that drew Marti to her job 12 years ago. Previously, while living in Hawaii, Marti had been a preschool teacher. When she moved to Oregon, she found no opportunities for work in that field. She had some secretarial abilities (typing, calculator, and telephone skills), and she wanted to continue working with people. At Peace Health, she found the perfect match.

Marti's personality and character equip her for her job very well. Her commitment in work (and in her life outside of work) is to one *Pillar of Character* in particular: Respect for Others. Her desire to listen to others' views is especially helpful when patients are in distress over bills that they might not be able to pay. Sometimes the distress comes across as anger. Marti describes her reaction:

"I meet all different types of people. I don't agree with some of their 'styles,' but nonetheless I must treat them non-judgmentally and put my own feelings aside. . . . It is very important to be able to listen and maintain my own sense of calm. This ability tends to calm them down too."

"It is possible to be both warm and caring and professional."

This Respect for Others was **instilled** in Marti as a child. As she says, "Both my parents stressed the importance of accepting all people on their own merits—not judging by looks, culture, etc."

Marti received other important lessons growing up as a Native American. She is very

interested in helping the next generation learn and preserve Native American traditions. For example, she volunteers for the Indian Education Program, working to build awareness and pride in children. She is also a traditional dancer. She and her husband participate in pow wows—singing, dancing, and drumming the music of their ancestors.

In all aspects of her life—whether at work or at play—Marti Martin always "walks her talk." She encourages young people like you to grow strong in your own commitments. When you believe in yourself and honor others, she says, the rest of life will fall into place.

Critical Thinking

1. How did Marti find her work as Customer Service Representative for the Billing Office?
2. How does Marti Martin go beyond being a secretary or bill collector?
3. In what ways did Marti's parents help shape her character and prepare her for her career?
4. How would you describe Marti Martin's character?

Respect for Others

Patricia M. Nagorski

Human Resources Consultant

While growing up in Ohio, Patricia Nagorski set her sights on becoming a teacher. After high school she attended a community college, and then went on to Cleveland State University. There she earned a degree in education and another degree in psychology. As she says, "My original career goal was to teach and then become a school psychologist." She seemed to be moving exactly in that direction.

After graduating from college, however, Nagorski found herself not teaching, but helping people with physical and mental challenges to find jobs. This was the beginning of her work in human resources. As she says, the field has much to do with solving problems: "helping employers spend their financial resources in ways that motivate employees to achieve the goals of the company (i.e., increased **revenue**, quality, timeliness)." Solving problems means helping people—and that's what Nagorski loves about her job.

Since she first began working in human resources, Nagorski has continuously prepared herself to meet the demands of her job. She went back to school, earning a masters degree in labor relations and human resources. She reads constantly in order to remain up-to-date on new laws and to understand their impact on employers and employees. She also participates in organizations of people who work in her field. Pat recommends to those individuals considering human resources, that they also concentrate on the areas of business and accounting. This is because a human resources person needs to become a **strategic** business partner with the total organization.

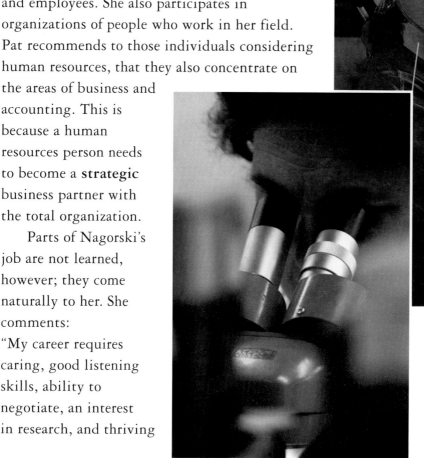

Parts of Nagorski's job are not learned, however; they come naturally to her. She comments: "My career requires caring, good listening skills, ability to negotiate, an interest in research, and thriving

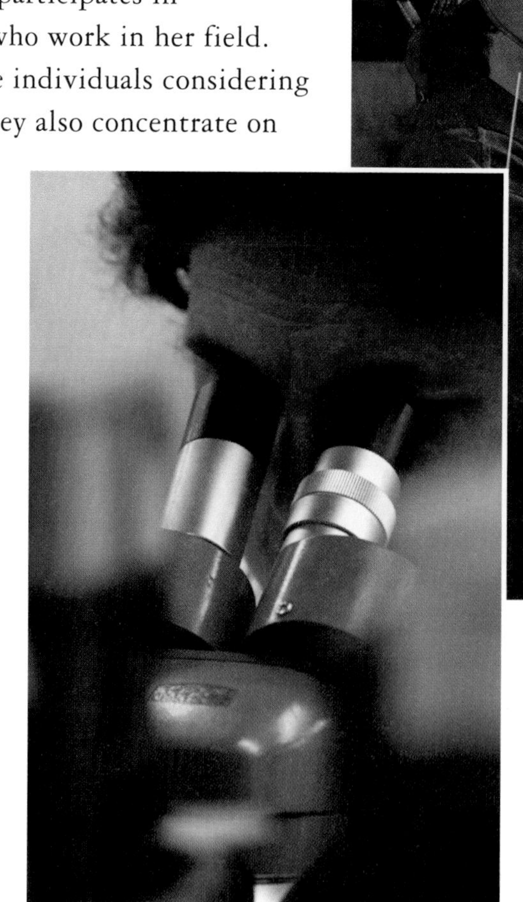

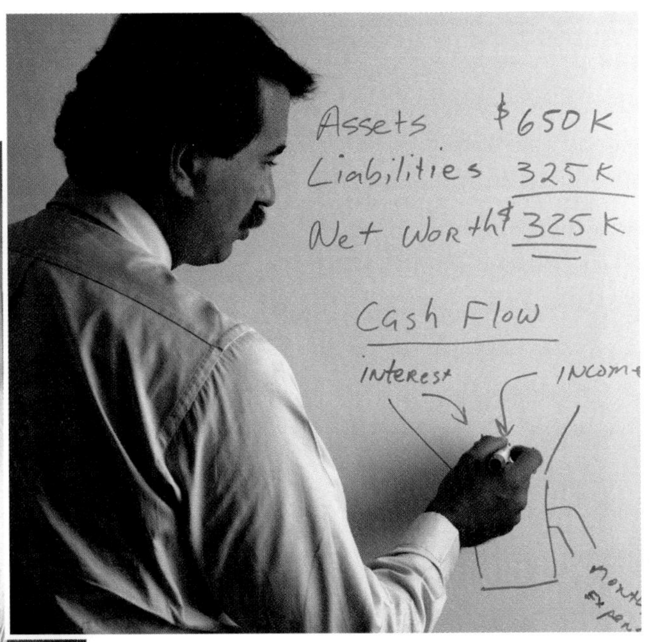

on challenge. . . all of which match my personality."

Nagorski also stresses the importance of the character trait Responsibility. She points out that in school and beyond, accountability and excellence are priceless tools. She would add one more component to the list—helping others. As Patricia Nagorski well knows, assisting others helps you feel good about yourself.

> **"My career requires caring, good listening skills, ability to negotiate, an interest in research, and thriving on challenge."**

Critical Thinking

1. What did Patricia originally study?
2. In what ways does Patricia's work as a human resources consultant involve problem solving?
3. In what ways has Nagorski prepared for her work in human resources?
4. How would you describe Patricia M. Nagorski's character?

Responsibility

Group Project

Making a Banner

Work with a group of four or five students to make banners. One purpose of this project is to celebrate working in an office, so as you proceed, consider what you might enjoy about that. You will be working with images and symbols to create your banners, so think of objects that you identify with office work. These could range from fairly obvious ones, such as a computer mouse on a cord, to fairly specialized ones such as an architect's compass. Decide as a group on a particular type of office to celebrate in your banner. Remember to use your best character traits as you work with your group.

Materials — fabric pieces, streamers, dowels, fabric glue, OR white paper, construction paper, tempera paint and brushes, colored markers, scissors, glue

Method — Choose whether you will be making a fabric banner or a paper banner. Sketch designs for the symbols you want to include. Decide on the colors you will use. Many flags and banners use one or more of seven basic colors: white, black, red, yellow, blue, green, and orange. Bright contrasting colors show up best from a distance. Design the banner, including the placement of your symbols. It is best not to use words but to let the symbols speak their meaning visually. Work together to create your banner. Attach your completed banner to a dowel and display it with pride.

I Work in an Office

Literature

Office

Wanda Coleman

for Fred Pollack

there the time clock's feverish ticks
there the bulging files full of static information
awaiting application
there the sturdy metal desk, upon it the word processor
with computer terminal and disc storage compartment
multiple metal filing trays, reference books
a pencil sharpener, pen & pencil holder, calendar
stapler, ashtray full of knick-knacks & paper clips
in-and-out trays, an anti-glare desk lamp
transcriber/dictator machine with special lite-wear
earphones, a box of snotkins, a half-eaten
chewy caramel nut bar, a cold cup of coffee grown over
with bacteria

a monster has eaten the secretary in this picture

intense focus on small things
keeps sane

Thinking and Journaling

You can just see this office. There's no beautiful mahogany desk with a leather chair here. Rather, it's a metal desk, metal filing trays. So much work goes on, but it doesn't seem to get anywhere; the files bulge with "static," or unmoving, information. There are a few concessions to comfort—none of them are very comforting, however. Suddenly we get the surprising news: the secretary is gone, eaten by a monster. The monster of monotony, the monster of repetition as endless as the clock's ticking, has gobbled up the inner life of the secretary. But someone remains to remember that focusing on small things, as the poem does, helps you stay sane. Or does it?

Many people who love their work find themselves spending all day in an office. If you work in an office, what will help you stay sane? What things and people could add meaning and charm to your work? Write your thoughts and feelings in your journal.

Writing

Science Fiction

Description Science fiction comes in many forms. Often it portrays an imagined technology, some mastermind machine that can save time if not save humanity. The reader of sci fi must "suspend disbelief," or not try to force the story into everyday logic. But the story has a logic of its own; it has internal consistency. It may even hypothesize about the future of humanity, often with a strong vision of hope.

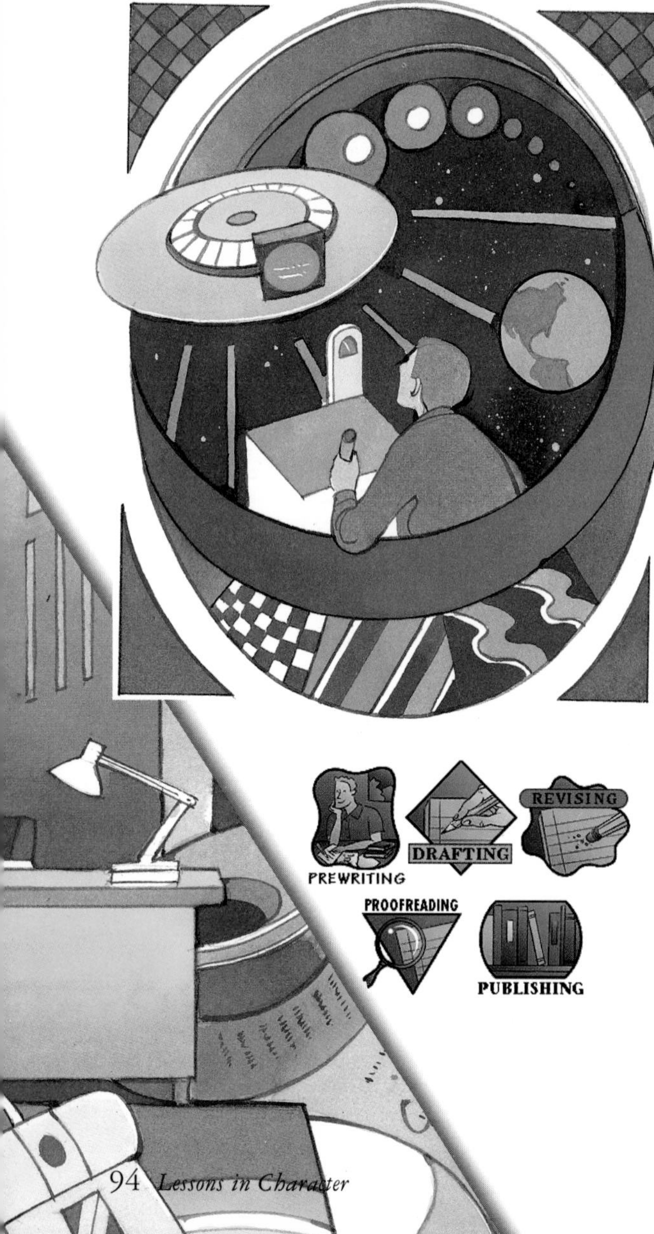

No matter how wildly imaginative it is, science fiction needs to show a sense of consistency. Science fiction often:

- Portrays a helpful new technology.
- Gives detailed descriptions of the machine or whatever it is.
- Includes at least one character who believes in the technology.

Assignment Your mission is to create a new technology that will forever change something involved in office work—and write a short science fiction story about it. Imagine yourself working in a particular kind of office, and then brainstorm until you come up with the best previously unknown technological wonder machine. Perhaps you are the inventor persuading other people to believe in your invention. Or perhaps you test out your new invention and it surprises you. Or perhaps some bold whippersnapper invents something that outwits your machine. But chances are you'll come up with a plot twist all your own.

Purposes to entertain, to describe an imagined technology in a convincing way

Audience your classmates

My Work as a Student

Pair Share

Careers — Work with a partner. Each of you will choose one of the people in this unit. Review the work that each person does. Then compare their work. In what ways is it similar? In what ways is it different? (Think about training, practice, place of work, and so on.)

What are you learning at school that would help you prepare for similar careers?

Character — *Responsibility* is the character trait Sanjay Jani stresses as most important in his work as an architect. In what ways can you relate responsibility to your work at school? (You might think about considering consequences before acting, thinking for the long term, being accountable, doing your best, and being disciplined.) List the many ways you are responsible in your life at school.

How can you tell when you are being responsible? What feelings do you feel? What thoughts do you think?

Set a goal of a new way you want to be responsible at school in the near future.

I Work with People
UNIT SIX

The words below, from Great People of the 20th Century *(a book put together by* Time *magazine's editors), are about Nelson Mandela. He is the man who fought for racial justice in South Africa, even while imprisoned for 27 years. He is the man who became the first black President of South Africa in 1994. Read to see what this amazing man, a man born to a royal family, is really like.*

When he speaks at banquets, he makes a point of going into the kitchen and shaking hands with every busboy. When he lived underground [in hiding from apartheid authorities] in the early 1960s and wanted to elude the police, his colleagues marveled at how he blended in with the people. He usually disguised himself as a chauffeur; he would don a long dustcoat, hunch his shoulders, and suddenly this tall, singularly regal figure was transformed into one of the huddled masses along the streets of Johannesburg. Even today, at rallies or meetings, the poorest South African feels he has the right to greet and address his leader.

Truly, Nelson Mandela is a man who loves people—all kinds of people. Are you like this too? Do you enjoy meeting people, talking, laughing, and sharing stories with them? Is your worst nightmare the feeling of loneliness?

If so, you probably would enjoy a job that allows you to work with people. Although all jobs involve some contact with others, certain careers are especially focused on dealing with the public.

In this unit, you will meet four individuals whose jobs revolve around people. Far from being president of a country, these workers nonetheless have the good character that makes them effective leaders in their own right.

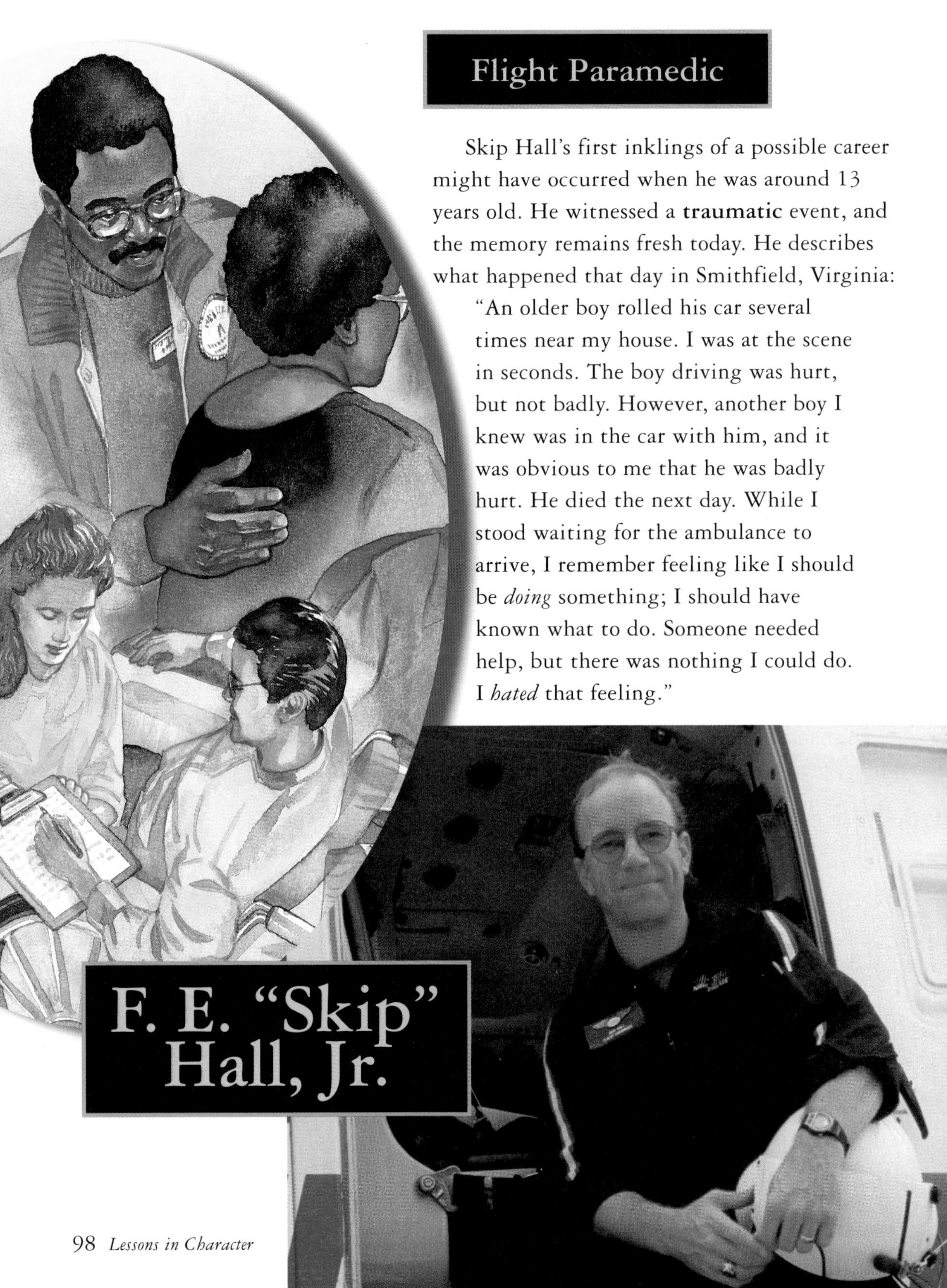

Flight Paramedic

Skip Hall's first inklings of a possible career might have occurred when he was around 13 years old. He witnessed a **traumatic** event, and the memory remains fresh today. He describes what happened that day in Smithfield, Virginia:

> "An older boy rolled his car several times near my house. I was at the scene in seconds. The boy driving was hurt, but not badly. However, another boy I knew was in the car with him, and it was obvious to me that he was badly hurt. He died the next day. While I stood waiting for the ambulance to arrive, I remember feeling like I should be *doing* something; I should have known what to do. Someone needed help, but there was nothing I could do. I *hated* that feeling."

F. E. "Skip" Hall, Jr.

Some 25 years later, Skip Hall usually *can* do something to help people who are injured. Since high school he has been involved in emergency medicine. It has never lost its attraction for him. As he says:

> "I was a volunteer rescue squad member in high school. I liked the excitement and unpredictability, and it felt 'right' to be helping people. I started college intending to go to medical school, but I was too impatient for that. I came home and worked my way through the certification process level by level until I reached paramedic."

In 1996, Skip's 20-year pursuit of a college education culminated in a degree. He graduated **summa cum laude** (with a nearly perfect grade point average) from Hampton University.

"Think about *the* world, not just *your* world."

Perhaps as important as Hall's training and education is his attitude toward people. He exhibits the character traits Caring and Responsibility in his work every day. As he says, "Caring makes you able to do this job at all and Responsibility ensures you will do it well."

That Hall truly *does* care about his patients is evident in his comments about his work. He considers himself a better person when he is able to help people through a tragic event. He likes the feeling he gets when he finds himself "running in when everyone else is running out." He sleeps well at night because he cares enough about every patient to give that person his very best. He translates this caring attitude into a

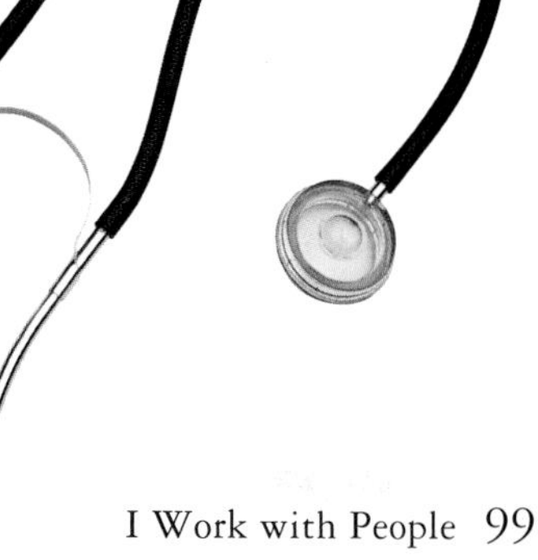

clear bit of advice for students like you: "Think about *the* world, not just *your* world. What can you do *today* that you will want to remember when you are 20, or 40, or 80? Do just one thing like that every day, whenever you can. You *will* make a difference, and the world will be a better place because you were here."

An example of Hall following this advice is his service on a three-year study as part of the Child Fatality Review Team. Commissioned by the governor of Virginia in 1995 to participate in this study, Skip feels "very proud" of the opportunity. He and the other members of the team are working to find new ways to save children's lives and keep them safe. Surely the results will make a difference, so that the world is a little better. For Skip Hall, that would be his ultimate dream come true.

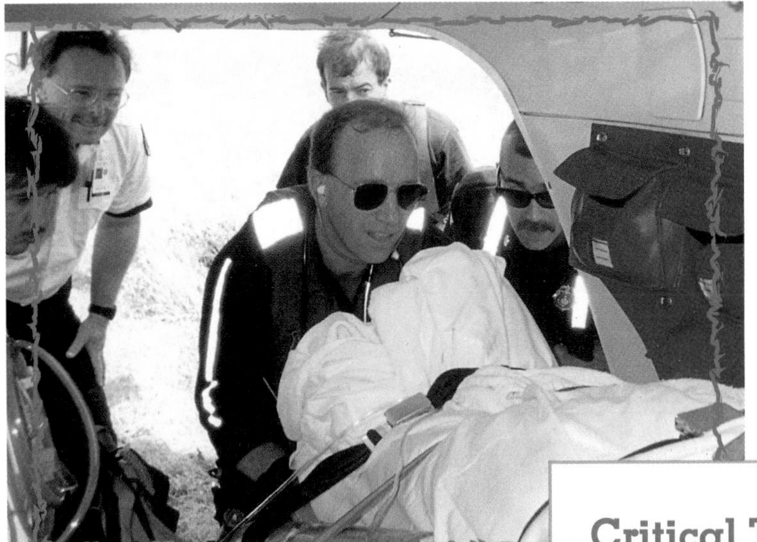

Critical Thinking

1. How did Skip become interested in being a paramedic?
2. How did Skip Hall prepare for his career, beginning in high school?
3. How would you describe F.E. "Skip" Hall, Jr.'s character?
4. What is a further service that Hall is doing in addition to his work?

Caring

Responsibility

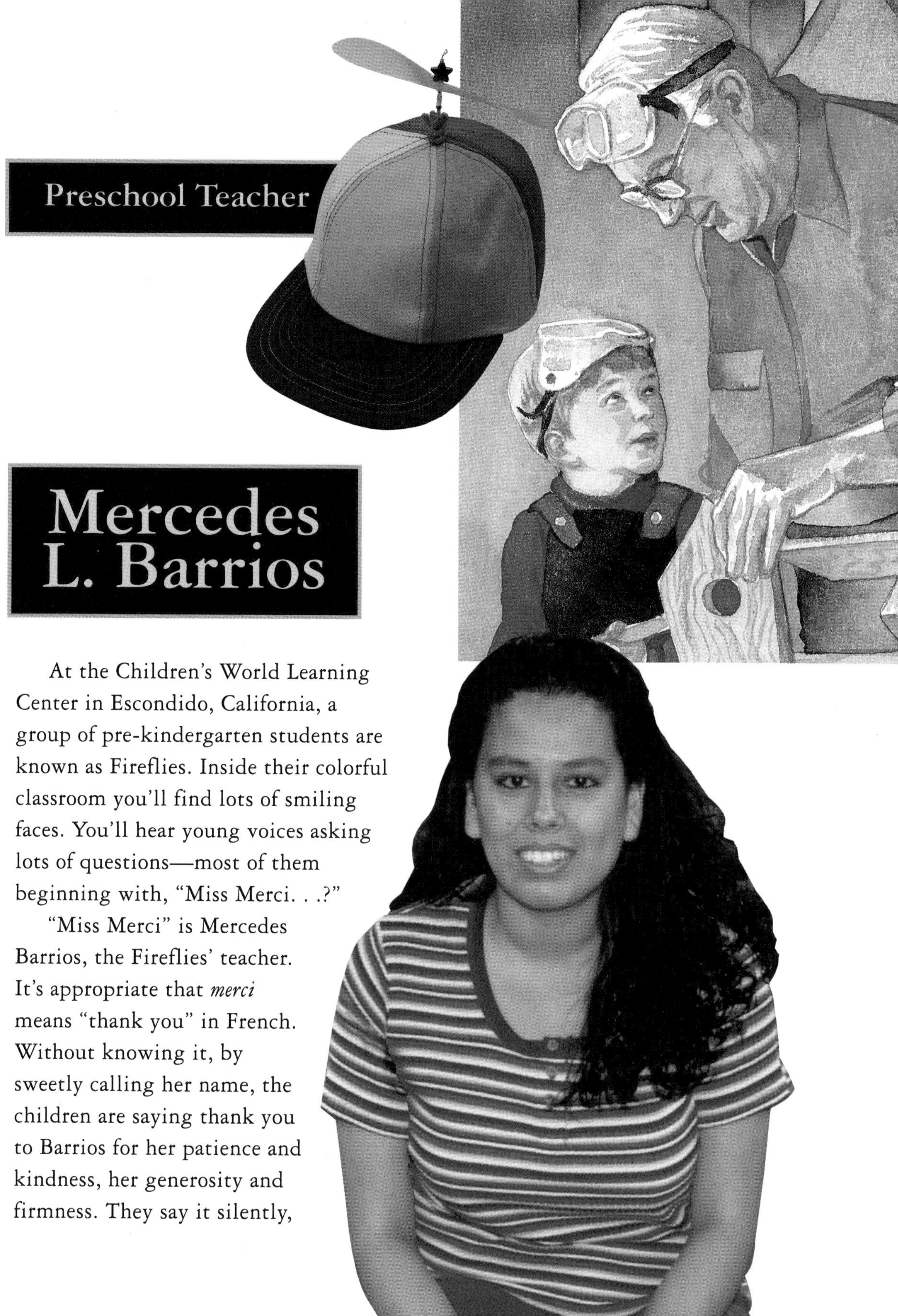

Preschool Teacher

Mercedes L. Barrios

At the Children's World Learning Center in Escondido, California, a group of pre-kindergarten students are known as Fireflies. Inside their colorful classroom you'll find lots of smiling faces. You'll hear young voices asking lots of questions—most of them beginning with, "Miss Merci. . .?"

"Miss Merci" is Mercedes Barrios, the Fireflies' teacher. It's appropriate that *merci* means "thank you" in French. Without knowing it, by sweetly calling her name, the children are saying thank you to Barrios for her patience and kindness, her generosity and firmness. They say it silently, too, Mercedes points out, with "the hugs and all of the cute things they do and say."

Mercedes Barrios has been a preschool teacher for all of her working life. She is very straightforward about why she likes it so much: "I enjoy making a difference in children's lives." She chose this area early—in the ninth grade. She remembers one teacher who was especially encouraging to her:

> "She was very laid back. When you needed someone to talk to, she was there to talk. She encouraged me to take child development classes."

"Be the best that you can be. Stay in school."

Barrios followed this advice, attending a community college in southern California to take the required courses. Since she began teaching, she has been named "teacher of the quarter" three different times. Her artistic and creative talents, along with her patience, are used daily on the job.

Barrios also uses something else daily—the character trait Respect for Others. This is especially important to her in dealing with the parents of her students. As she explains: "Everyone has their own ways of doing things. I wouldn't want to interfere."

When the 5-year-olds she teaches now grow up to be your age, Mercedes Barrios might still be busy answering "Miss Merci. . . ?" questions. However, her advice to them—and to you—will never change: "Be the best that you can be. Stay in school." Thanks to Miss Merci, a certain group of children with the distinctive name Fireflies are off to a good start.

Critical Thinking

1. How did Mercedes decide to become a preschool teacher?
2. How did Barrios prepare for her career?
3. How would you describe Mercedes L. Barrios's character?
4. What advice does Barrios give to you as a student?

Respect for Others

Realtor

In 1989, Gordon Brown decided to make a career change. After seven years in banking, he was ready for a new challenge. He wanted more opportunities for personal growth and creativity. But what field could match his desires?

To find the answer, first Gordon looked at his job experience. For the last several years, he had been helping people get loans for homes. He knew a great deal about this type of financial commitment.

Brown also took a look at his interests outside of work. His extensive community involvement meant that he had a real interest in seeing people happily settled in the area of Kalamazoo, Michigan.

Gordon Brown

Finally, Brown explored his special talents. His ability to communicate well with others and to build positive relationships meant he wanted to continue working with people.

All of these things, when added together, pointed to one field that would be a very good match for Gordon Brown: **real estate**. This is the area he decided to pursue.

With this decision made, Brown's first move was to take a real estate class. The purpose of such a class is to prepare a person to pass an exam and become licensed as a realtor. Brown passed the test easily. But he didn't stop there. He went right to work as a realtor, and continued on to earn the Graduate Realtor Institute (GRI) designation in 1993. This award honored Gordon's exceptional training and experience in real estate sales.

Brown is happy to share his knowledge with others. He writes articles and gives seminars on real estate topics. He makes himself available to his clients and to his community. These actions fit with the *Pillar of Character* he selects as most important to him in achieving success: Citizenship. As he explains: "Community service gave me a means to expand my skills and establish a wide-ranging network of friends that I would have not otherwise been able to do. All this happened while I was able to be of help to others who were in need."

Gordon Brown's success began, in a large part, when he was a student like you. At that time, he read as much as he could—especially biographies. As he puts it, "I wanted to learn all I could about what I needed to do to be a success in life." He encourages you, too, to seek information—to have an "inquiring mind."

"I wanted to learn all I could about what I needed to do to be a success in life."

Critical Thinking

1. How did Gordon decide on his second career?
2. How did Brown prepare for his career in real estate?
3. How would you describe Gordon Brown's character?
4. How did reading biographies help Gordon?

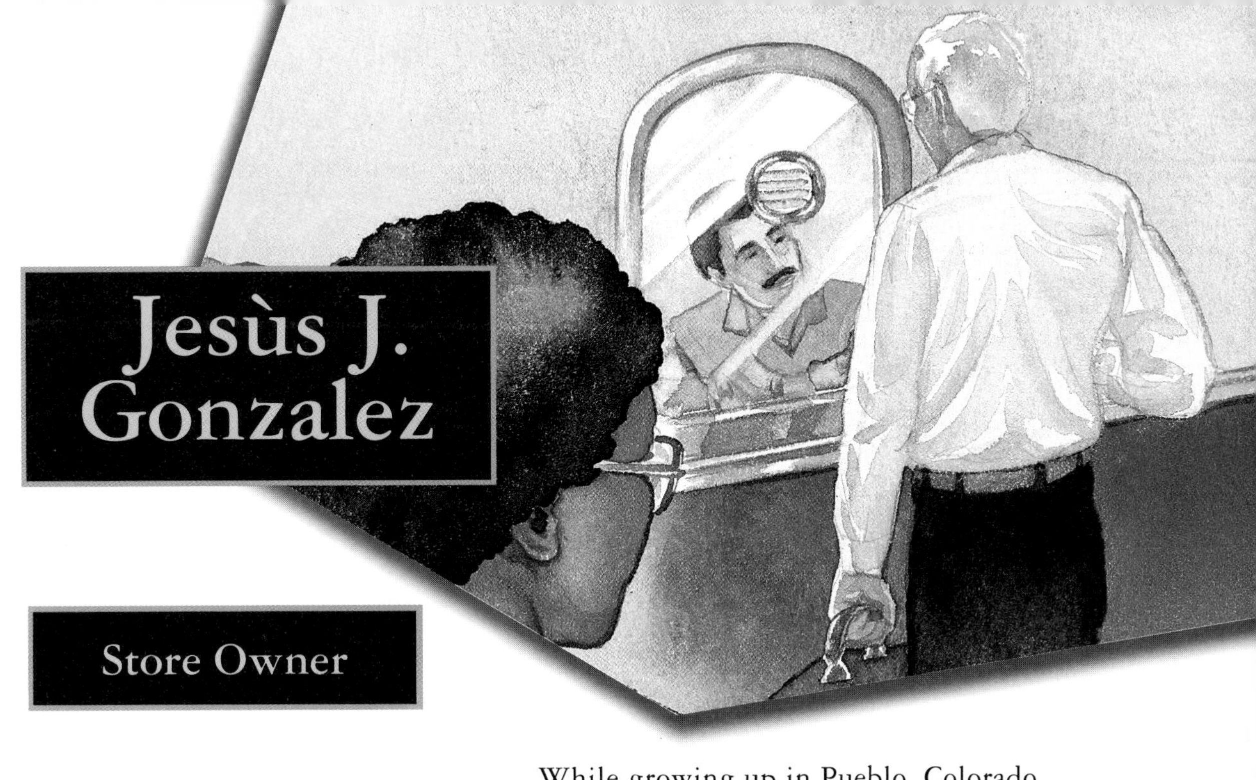

Jesùs J. Gonzalez

Store Owner

While growing up in Pueblo, Colorado, Jesùs ("Jess") Gonzalez strongly felt the love and support of his family. He recalls how his parents encouraged him to participate in a variety of activities. This helped him to meet many different people, to make new friends, who were always welcome in the Gonzalez home.

Today, as the owner of La Casa Basket and Gift Company in Lewisville, Texas, Jess is happily using the talents and values

"I'm always trying to make people aware of how to care more for each other."

that were nurtured when he was a child. For example, his ease with people makes him comfortable with the sales aspect of his business. His Respect for Others (the character trait he feels is most important to him at work) means he has good relationships with his customers. And the flexibility afforded him because he owns his own business means Gonzalez can participate in the activities he feels are most important in life: family and community involvement.

It was his commitment to community service and his desire for more family time that led Gonzalez some four years ago to give up his job as a telecommunications account specialist to make the leap to the **retail** industry. In the beginning, he ran the store out of his home. After two years, he was on such solid ground that he was able to open La Casa in a Lewisville shopping mall. The store specializes in handmade items of cultural significance. Gonzalez loves the merchandise and describes the most enjoyable part of his job this way: ". . . dealing with people directly and selling items

“There are two things guaranteed in life, peaks and valleys.”

I like and believe in, especially cultural items." Offering such merchandise helps Gonzalez promote cultural awareness.

Away from the store, Gonzalez is committed to a **nonprofit** organization that he helped to found: *Para Los Ninos* ("For the Kids"). The main goal of this organization is to keep at-risk high school students in school. Jess and his wife, Audrey, spend many hours weekly working for this cause. Their teenage son is also involved, so while doing this important community service, Gonzalez also gains cherished family time.

When asked what advice he offers to students, Gonzalez has this to say: "There are two things guaranteed in life, peaks and valleys. Valleys may be hard or painful, but out of them emerges a better person."

In Lewisville, Texas, at least, there are people to help those in need travel up toward the peaks. Those people are the Gonzalez family.

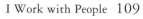

Critical Thinking

1. What did his parents do that helped Jess become the person he is?
2. What work does Jess do now?
3. What is the main goal of Jess's nonprofit organization, *Para Los Ninos?*
4. How would you describe Jesùs J. Gonzalez's character?

Respect for Others

Group Project

Creating a Bulletin Board

Work with a group of four or five students to create a bulletin board. One purpose of this activity is to work with people, so as you are working, reflect about the process. Might you enjoy this kind of career? Your bulletin board should be designed to celebrate a career that involves working with people. Choose a career that you have not explored yet, to broaden your thinking. What are the various roles people play? Are there bosses or not? Where does the work take place?

Remember to use your best character traits as you work with your group.

Materials — construction paper, aluminum foil, art tissue, corrugated cardboard, fabric scraps, crepe paper, ribbons, colored markers, glue, tape, magazine pictures, found objects, thumb tacks, a stapler

Method — Decide what type of bulletin board you want: realistic, symbolic, whimsical, or some combination of types. For example, if you are doing a bulletin board to celebrate people who work in a circus, you might include art to represent the three rings and the performers, and also real objects such as a soft drink cup, a silly hat, a whistle, and so on. Aim for flamboyance!

I Work with People

Bosses

Tom Wayman *after Nicanor Parra*

The boss who stands behind you
watching you work.
The boss who insists
"I'm sure I told you to do that."
The boss who, after you've made nine trips
carrying an extra-heavy load of boards,
sees you walking with a light load
and tells your foreman to order you to work harder.
The boss who commands you to look busy.

The foreman who can't resist showing you a better way.
The foreman who won't let you
do something a better way.
The one who is also head
of the union's grievance committee.
The foreman who is unable or forgot to
requisition enough parts
and orders you to "make do with what you have."

The supervisor who is afraid
of the boss.
The supervisor in love with memos.
The supervisor who checks the washroom
to be certain no one is there too long.
The new supervisor who doesn't understand
    what is happening
and so concentrates on enforcing regulations
everybody forgot about years ago.

These bosses
in their coats and ties
with their specially colored hard hats, their offices,
watches, clipboards,
with their ulcers
and their pathetic attempts to appear calm
are, by and large,
totally useless.

Thinking and Journaling

Working with people brings problems and joys, just like living with people or going to school with them. Clearly this poet has had some useless bosses!

How would you like to be a boss? What might you like about it? What might you dislike? Write your thoughts and feelings in your journal.

Writing

Editorials

Description

"Rock music is ruining our children." "Everyone should have to read the classics." "Our chocolate worms will make you popular." "The driving age should be raised to 20." Sound funny, yet familiar? No doubt you are bombarded by opinions and advertising from media and probably from those you know and love. Persuasion comes in many forms; one of the sanest is editorials. People, many of whom are not professional writers, express their opinions and sometimes try to persuade other readers to agree with them.

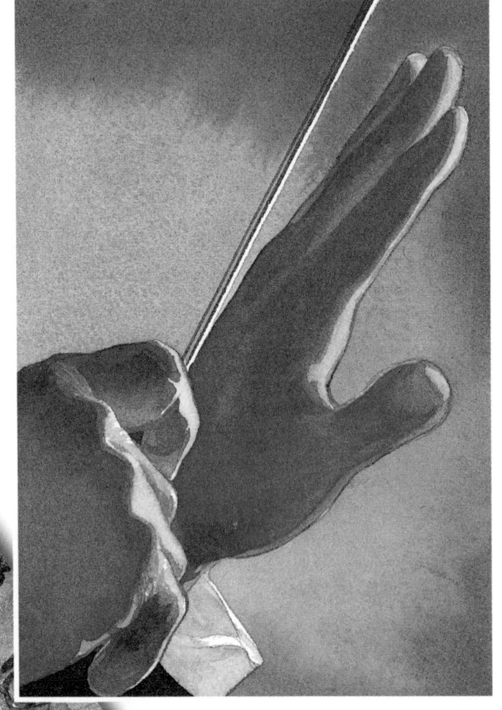

Editorials, letters to the editor, and "op ed" pieces are similar ways of expressing opinions. Editorials often:

- State a clear point of view on one topic.
- Give facts and opinions to back up the point.
- Include logical reasons rather than appeals to emotion.

Assignment

Using the writing process, write an editorial or a letter to the editor of your school or local paper. Think of a question that worries and interests you. Choose one that has to do with people at school, such as a problem about sports, classes, lunch, or friends. Get a clear idea of your audience, what they already know and believe about your topic. Write a clear statement of your opinion. You might want to make a simple outline of a reason followed by facts, another reason followed by facts, and so on. One way to end your editorial is with a call to action. As you write, be wary of appeals to emotion; appeals to reason show more respect for your reader.

PREWRITING DRAFTING REVISING PROOFREADING PUBLISHING

Purposes to persuade, to express ideas

Audience your classmates, or adults

My Work as a Student

Pair Share

Careers — Work with a partner. Each of you will choose one of the people in this unit. Review the work that each person does. Then compare their work. In what ways is it similar? In what ways is it different? (Think about training, practice, place of work, and so on.)

What are you learning at school that would help you prepare for similar careers?

Character — *Citizenship* is a character trait Gordon Brown emphasizes in his work as a realtor. He reminds us how important it is to contribute to our community. In what ways can you relate citizenship to your work at school? (You might think about actions such as following rules, doing your share, protecting the environment, and respecting authority.) List the many ways you are a good citizen in your life at school.

How can you tell when you are being a good citizen? What feelings do you feel? What thoughts do you think?

Set a goal of a new way you want to be a good citizen at school in the near future.

Citizenship

0 1 0 1 1 1 0 1 0 0 0 0 1
Welcome to
Prime
Universe!
I Work
with
Computers
PLANET: MIKO
UNIT SEVEN

from The Gadget Factor

Sandy Landsman

The main character of this novel is Michael Goldman, a 13-year-old mathematical genius. He is so smart that he is already in college! It's there that he meets a new friend, his roommate Worm, who gets him really interested in computers for the first time. As you'll see below, by Chapter 2, Michael is so in love with computers that he hardly thinks about anything else.

One night, lying in bed, I got a brainstorm. I was thinking about Plato's *Republic*—kind of an early utopia I'd read for Poli Sci at the beginning of the term—and wondered what it would be like to program on a computer the government described. I began mapping out in my mind a flow chart for a general plan of attack, when it hit me: if this could be programmed, why not more? Why restrict it to just a plan of government? We could include an ecosystem, a whole planet... and more. Just a flash of an idea—and suddenly I was awake, as excited as I'd ever been. It reminded me of the time at the age of nine when I first intuited what geometric proofs were all about and set out to prove every theorem in the book in two sleepless, exhilarating nights. Only this was even better—the scope so much more sublime.

"Worm?"

"Yeah?"

"Why don't we invent our own computer game?"

He sat up in bed. I could sense a grin spreading on his face. "Yes—yes, that would be a challenge. Very complex to do, if we do it right. I mean, unless we do another computer tic-tac-toe or something trivial like that, but if we do it right..."

My toes tingled. "Worm—what I'm thinking of isn't trivial."

"You thought of a premise?"

"Yes." I waited a minute, drawing out the effect.

"Well? Come on!"

"Supposing—supposing we could program our own universe?"

"Our own universe?"

"Galaxies, planets, the laws of physics—with just a few strategic differences from the laws of physics in this universe, that might enable, say, a practical form of time travel or whatever else we decide we'll

want to do in the new universe. And one community in particular. And people—we can give them names and characteristics, set them in action. . . A whole universe in a computer!" The scope of the project floored me.

For once, Worm was silent, too. At last he laughed. "Mike, you're a megalomaniac! It's tempting—it's very tempting—but we could never do it. It would take too much time—too many man-hours for us to write the programs, too many computer-hours to test it out and debug it and set it in motion."

I was ahead of him. "We'll incorporate existing programs—every computer game, every description of the physical and social universe that's ever been programmed, we'll tie them all up into the biggest game of all!"

Worm shook his head. "You're crazy—but I can't pass it up!"

I felt like jumping out of bed. "We'll call it. . . Universe Prime—our universe. With a Planet Miko and a village called the Worm Farm!"

"Run by a Worm who is brilliant and eccentric and true and a champion among earth burrowers!"

"And by Michael, who is strong and brave and tall and shrewd! Michael is the ruler, and Worm is his loyal helper."

"Hey!"

"Well, I thought of it!"

"Co-rulers. Co-rulers or I won't play."

I felt so good I conceded the point. "Co-rulers. With alternating six-month periods of ascendancy—mine first. And we'll rule benignly for our loyal subjects."

Already in my mind I was sketching out a plan of attack for the programming. The keyboard would be our instrument of control; and the print-out terminal would tell us the consequences of our actions and the fate of an entire universe—droughts, years of plenty, space travel, creatures from other worlds, the birth and death of a billion stars—all locked in the circuits of the IBM 3033. . . .

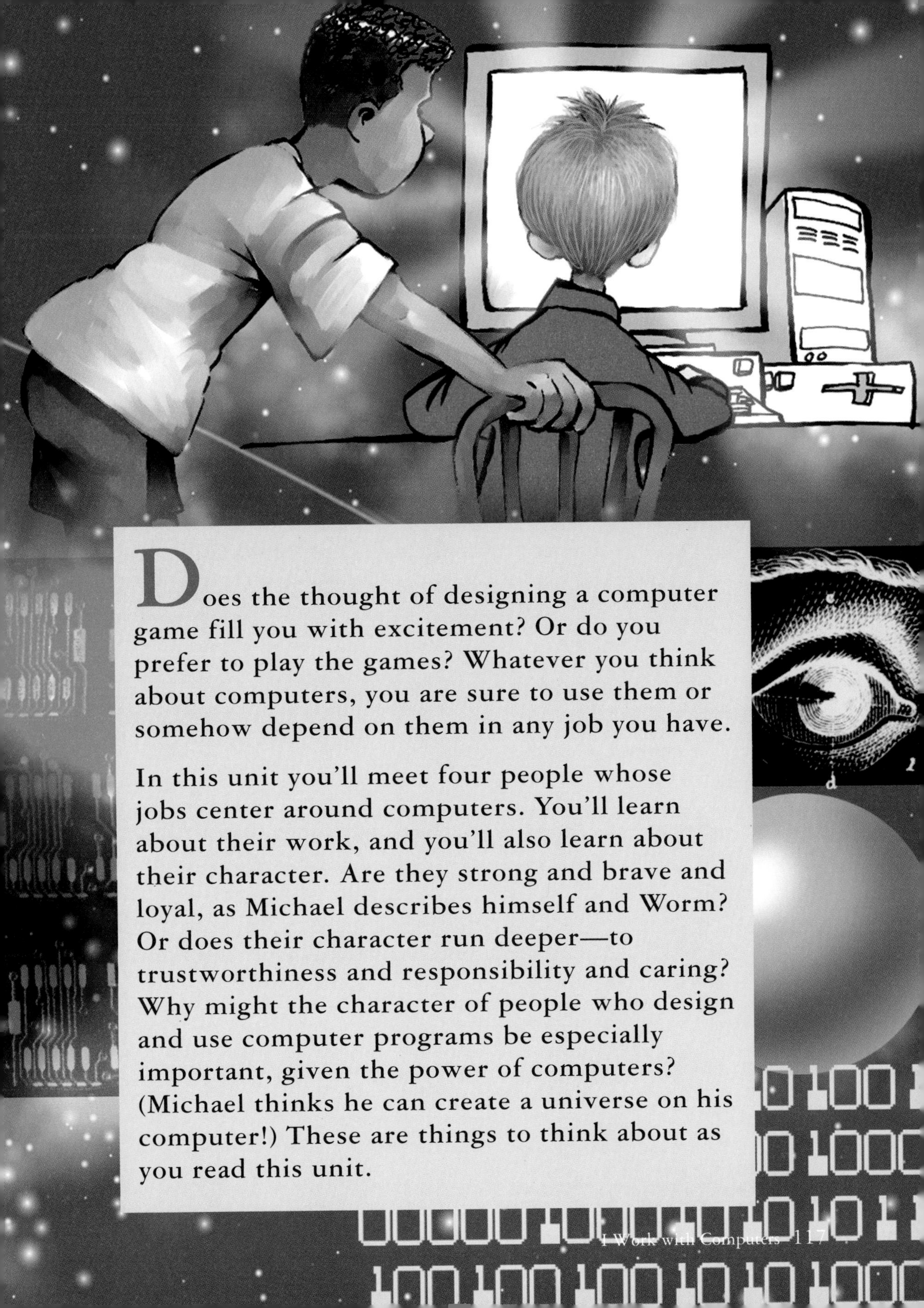

Does the thought of designing a computer game fill you with excitement? Or do you prefer to play the games? Whatever you think about computers, you are sure to use them or somehow depend on them in any job you have.

In this unit you'll meet four people whose jobs center around computers. You'll learn about their work, and you'll also learn about their character. Are they strong and brave and loyal, as Michael describes himself and Worm? Or does their character run deeper—to trustworthiness and responsibility and caring? Why might the character of people who design and use computer programs be especially important, given the power of computers? (Michael thinks he can create a universe on his computer!) These are things to think about as you read this unit.

Tracy Wieland

Web Site Designer

Tracy Wieland was led to her career by an extracurricular activity she participated in during high school: the making of the school yearbook. It was while working on the yearbook that she discovered her interest in (and talent for) design and layout. These two skills are at the heart of web site design.

Previously, Tracy had developed other artistic skills. In middle school, for example, she had an art teacher who meant a lot to her. Tracy says about her:

"Being fair is vital if you want to be a team player. . ."

"My art teacher was very positive and saw good in everything. She taught me that no matter what you choose to do, do your absolute best."

Tracy definitely has done her best to prepare for and achieve success in a field that is relatively new. After high school, she earned an associates degree in visual arts from a community college. While there, she worked as an **intern** for the college newspaper. For her efforts she received an Editors Excellence Award. Today, on the job at Ramshaw-Smith Company (a real estate firm) in Champaign, Illinois, Tracy challenges herself to keep up on the latest technology. This is what keeps her designs looking fresh and creative, helping her to meet both her personal and professional goals.

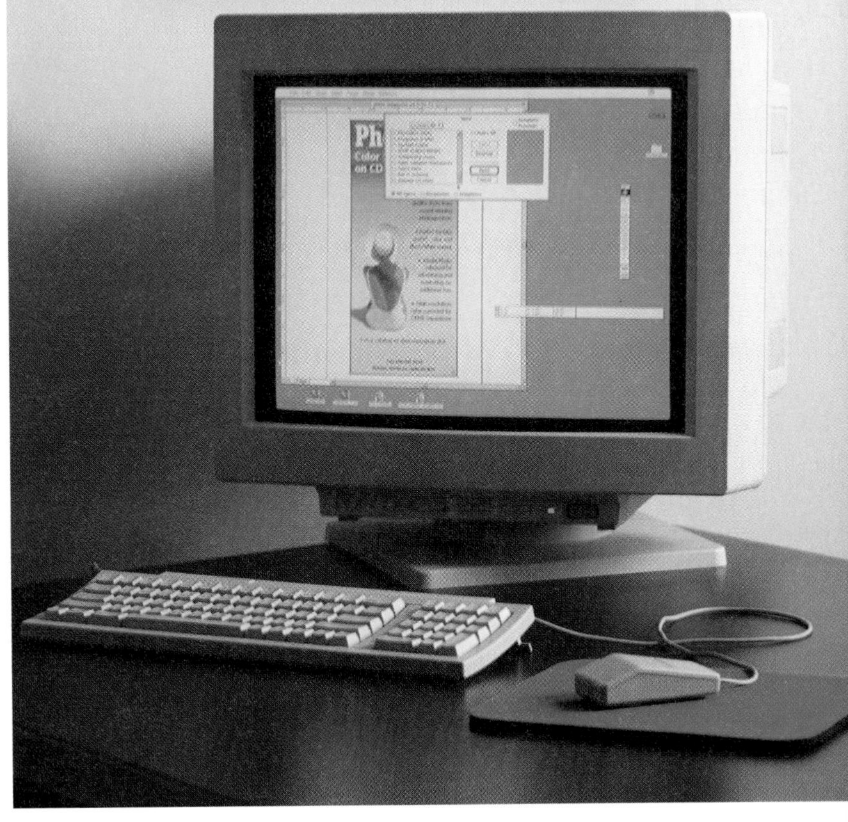

When asked about a character trait that is most important to her on the job, Tracy suggests Fairness: "Being fair is vital if you want to be a team player, which will help you accomplish more." Working with others, listening to their ideas, looking for new ways to present information. . . these are all important parts of Wieland's daily work. It helps that she views herself as a **flexible** person, someone who can "go with the flow" to help make things happen.

> "Do your best, and you'll never be disappointed."

To students like you, Tracy Wieland passes on the advice her art teacher once gave her: "Do your best, and you'll never be disappointed." She also wanted to leave you with these inspirational words of Dr. Martin Luther King, Jr.:

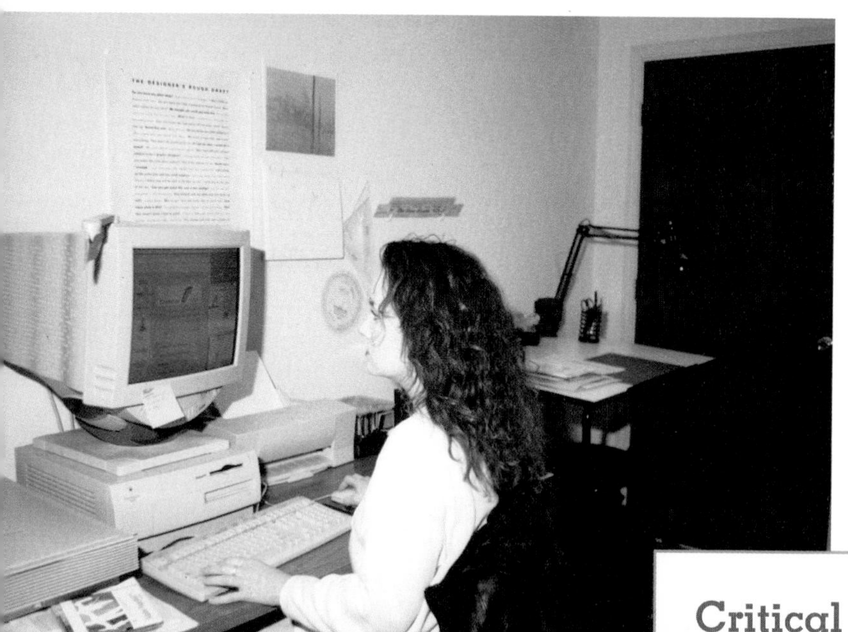

If a person sweeps streets for a living,
he should sweep them
as Michelangelo painted,
as Beethoven composed,
as Shakespeare wrote.

Critical Thinking

1. How did Tracy become interested in the field of design?
2. What training has Tracy had for her career as a web site designer?
3. How would you describe Tracy Wieland's character?
4. What are some other important parts of Wieland's daily work?

Fairness

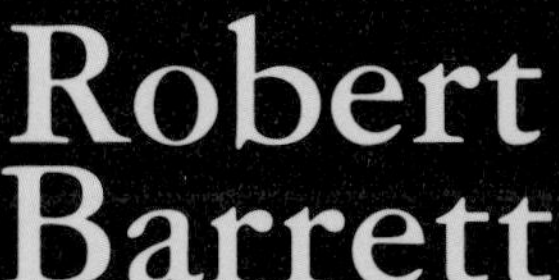

Robert Barrett

Computer Design Engineer

When you ask Robert Barrett important questions, his answers often come in twos. One answer balances and completes the other. Perhaps this has something to do with why he is such a successful engineer. After all, balance and completeness are very important parts of successful design.

Robert grew up in Millington, Tennessee, and by his senior year in high school he knew he wanted to pursue a college degree in electrical engineering. He gives two reasons for this choice, one serious and one rather funny: "I liked computers and electronics." and "Electrical Engineering had the least English requirements of any major in the Mississippi State University catalog." Clearly, Robert's enjoyment of math and science courses balanced out his dislike of English courses!

Today, on the job in Huntsville, Alabama, Robert

"No one pushed or pulled me toward being successful."

uses his engineering expertise to design **hardware**, the physical components of computers. His knowledge alone is not enough, however. It is accompanied by two important personality traits that Robert has. He explains: "It takes *patience* to complete a long project. I also use *communication skills* to get ideas across to everyone—from my superiors to production-line employees—so that I can solve problems, build and fix things."

When everything goes right, Robert Barrett knows the full joy of his job. When he "gets to see it work" he knows the processes of designing and building a project have been successful. Behind the success is always found a great deal of hard work.

Barrett learned the importance of hard work from a middle school math teacher who taught him that, "HARD work is necessary to learn HARD things." This advice was balanced in part by a second piece of

advice from a physics teacher who stressed that learning could be fun. Barrett offers his own twin pieces of advice to students like you: "WORK at school. LISTEN to your elders; they really do know more than you do."

When it comes to deciding on a *Pillar of Character* that most helped him get where he is today, however, Robert Barrett firmly settles on one answer: Responsibility. As he states, "No one pushed or pulled me toward being successful. It was MY responsibility to realize what I needed to do."

With these words, we do have a balanced and complete picture of Robert Barrett's success.

Responsibility

Critical Thinking

1. Why did Robert choose to major in electrical engineering?
2. What does Robert design in his work?
3. How does Robert know when he's been successful?
4. How would you describe Robert Barrett's character?

Welcome to
Prime
Universe!

Eldon Doty

Graphic Illustrator

It's been about three years since Eldon Doty laid down his paints and brushes and started doing his work as an artist on a computer. It was an amazing change. As Doty says, "I was blown away with the ability that the computer gives me in creativity and control over an illustration."

Having pulled himself back together, Doty now works regularly on the computer, producing marvelous images such as those appearing within this lesson and

"I've learned that if you really love doing something you will tend to practice at it very hard."

unit and throughout Unit Two as well. Take a look at these pictures. Eldon Doty defines himself as a humorous illustrator. Can you see why?

Doty's delight in all things funny began when he was a child. In school he was the "class clown," the one who would do nearly anything to get a laugh. When his funny drawings amused his classmates, he had the **incentive** he needed to keep drawing. The result was better pictures. As he points out:

> "Drawing is just like playing the piano—there is no magic to it—the more you practice the better you get. I've learned that if you really love doing something you will tend to practice at it very hard."

Drawing continued to be a fascinating, fun hobby for Eldon, even as he went to college, joined the Seattle Police Department, and served as an officer for 13 years. All the while, he kept drawing. He also took classes in graphic design and illustration. His ever-growing interest in the field finally led him to enroll in the San Francisco Academy of Art.

“It is important to stop and think about the job.”

Soon, Doty had so many jobs coming in that he decided to make illustration his full-time job! That was nearly 15 years ago. Today, Eldon Doty still enjoys being self-employed and has no problem finding work. He points out that a decision-making model like STAR helps him to remain focused on his clients' needs:

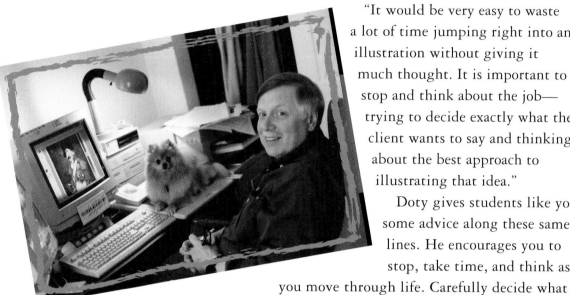

"It would be very easy to waste a lot of time jumping right into an illustration without giving it much thought. It is important to stop and think about the job—trying to decide exactly what the client wants to say and thinking about the best approach to illustrating that idea."

Doty gives students like you some advice along these same lines. He encourages you to stop, take time, and think as you move through life. Carefully decide what you really enjoy doing. Then, like Eldon Doty, "do it because you love it"—and concentrate on being the best at it.

Critical Thinking

1. What big change has Eldon made recently in his career as a graphic illustrator?
2. How has Eldon's sense of humor influenced his work?
3. What studies have helped Doty in his career as an illustrator?
4. How would you describe Eldon Doty's character?

STAR

Danny Sanchez

Computer Programmer

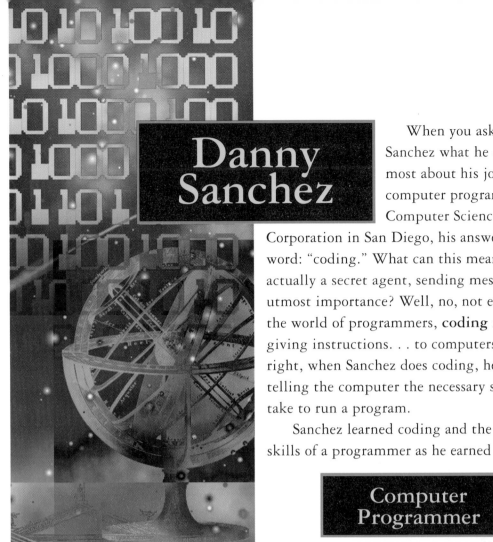

When you ask Danny Sanchez what he enjoys most about his job as a computer programmer for Computer Sciences Corporation in San Diego, his answer is one word: "coding." What can this mean? Is he actually a secret agent, sending messages of utmost importance? Well, no, not exactly. In the world of programmers, **coding** refers to giving instructions. . . to computers. That's right, when Sanchez does coding, he is telling the computer the necessary steps to take to run a program.

Sanchez learned coding and the other skills of a programmer as he earned his

college degree in computer information science. His commitment to the field goes back to his high school years in New Mexico, however, when he figured out how well computer sciences matched his interest in mathematics and **logic** (correct reasoning). Being a programmer also has turned out to match Danny's personality, as he explains: "Being a programmer takes patience. You must be thorough (meticulous) and devoted. Having a great attitude always helps because of the pressures involved."

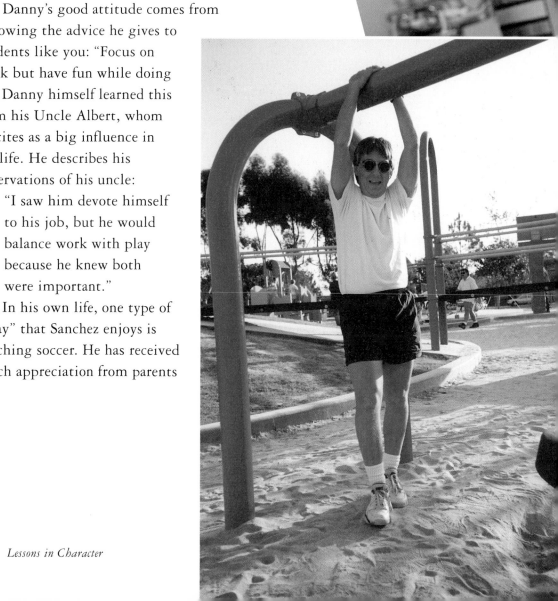

Danny's good attitude comes from following the advice he gives to students like you: "Focus on work but have fun while doing it." Danny himself learned this from his Uncle Albert, whom he cites as a big influence in his life. He describes his observations of his uncle:

> "I saw him devote himself to his job, but he would balance work with play because he knew both were important."

In his own life, one type of "play" that Sanchez enjoys is coaching soccer. He has received much appreciation from parents

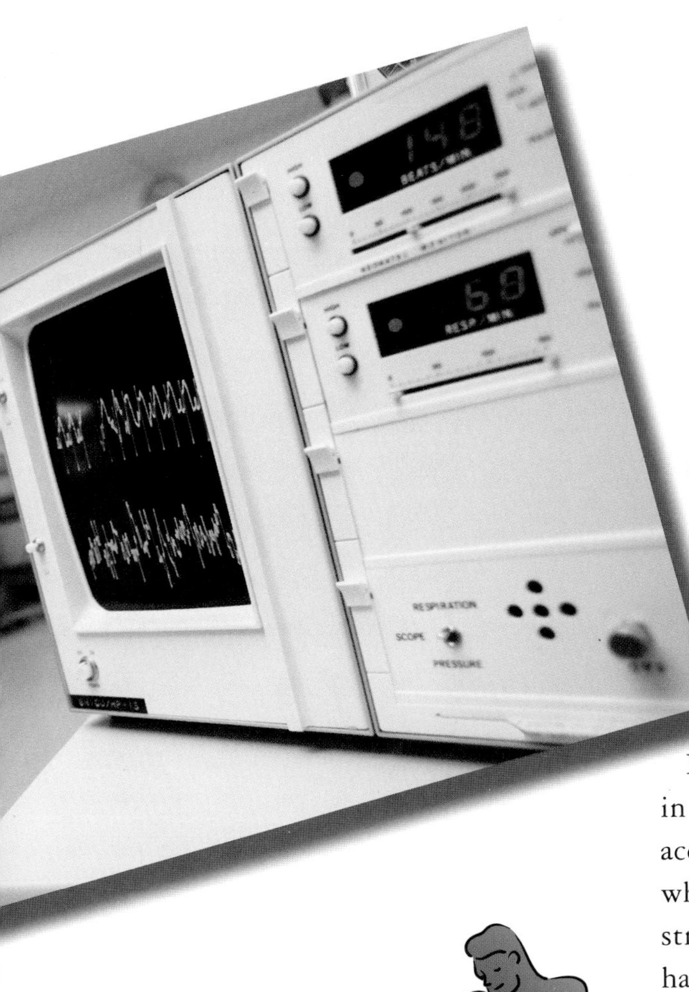

> “Focus on work but have fun while doing it.”

and players for his efforts over the past 10 years. This is very gratifying to him.

Whether at work or at play, Sanchez is committed to the character traits Trustworthiness and Responsibility. As he says, “I put in an honest day’s work, and I am accountable for the excellence of what I do.” He encourages you to strive for excellence also—and to have the self-discipline it takes to succeed.

Critical Thinking

1. What is coding?
2. What were Danny’s academic interests in high school?
3. What is one type of play that Danny enjoys?
4. How would you describe Danny Sanchez’s character?

Trustworthiness
Responsibility

Designing a Web Site

Work with a group of four or five students to design a computer game or a web site. One purpose of this activity is to consider how you would like working with computers as a career, so reflect on your thoughts and feelings.

Whether you choose to create a computer game or a web site, focus on the visual effects you can create. You will probably have text and audio in your design as well. Since your design will be on paper, you can use speech balloons to represent the audio. Use your imagination to come up with a design unlike any other you have seen.

Remember to use your best character traits as you work with your group.

Materials — large white paper, colored pens and markers, tempera paint or watercolors, magazine pictures, scissors, glue, colored paper or tissue, pencils, pens

Method — Decide which project you will do, a computer game or a web site. Brainstorm a list of components, stages, steps, sections, segments, surprises, all the elements you can think of. Then turn your ideas into a visual creation. You may want to set up the sequence of "screens" as a long comic strip or a film strip with individual frames. New ideas may come to you as you work, so include them as well. Also, you may find that some of your original ideas are impossible. You will need to be flexible.

I Work with Computers

Literature

Think Tank

Eve Merriam

Think thinktank THINK
get an inkling think tank
INPUT INPUT
increment increment INPUT
  increment
link the trunk line
line up the data bank
blink on the binary
don't play a prank
THINK tanktink THINK
don't go blank
don't leave us bleak
INPUT INPUT outflank
don't flunk out
thinktank THINK THINK
don't lack a link in
INPUT INPUT
don't sputter off NO NO
ON go on stronger
wangle an angle GO
thinktank THINK
don't put us out of luck stuck
on the brink
don't conk out
INPUT INPUT
something bungled
mangled rattled
RETHINK thinktank RETHINK
disentangle
unwrinkle
undo the junk CLUNK
plug up the CHINK the leak
don't peter out be fleet
be NEAT
we hunger for hanker for answer
print out print out print out
THANK you THINKTANK
  THANKTANK
THINK you TANKYOU out
  THINK
REPEAT REPEAT REPEAT
THANK YOU THINKTANK
THINK
TANK
DONE
THUNK.

Thinking and Journaling

What do you think!? Can't you just hear the machine in the words, making its motor noises, some LOUD, some soft? Does your brain ever feel like that?

How do you feel about working with computers? Are you ecstatic, intrigued, terrified? Why? What role do you think computers will play in your life? Write your thoughts and feelings in your journal.

Writing

Fantasy

Description A fantasy appeals to your sense of fun. Things that can't really happen, do happen. Creatures that don't really live, do live. Places that don't really exist, do exist. The characters, the dialogue, the descriptions all may be wildly or mildly exaggerated. Noble characters struggle to live up to their best potential, against odds that are beyond belief (and reality).

While the purpose of fantasy is usually to illuminate reality, fantasies sometimes:

- Portray characters that don't really exist.
- Take place in an "other-world" type of setting.
- Have supernatural elements like time travel.

Assignment Since computers first became popular, or known about at all, there have been rumors of these machines taking over our lives, our very world. Computers have been seen as the unknown, a possible enemy. Now is your chance to imagine the wildest things a computer might do. Your computer may have human or godlike powers. Surely there will be a hero or heroine to save humanity! Write a fantasy, perhaps one that is suitable for reading to a young child, about a computer. Remember to use the steps of the writing process as you work.

PREWRITING DRAFTING REVISING PROOFREADING PUBLISHING

Purposes to entertain, to evoke feelings, to describe something fantastic

Audience young children, or your classmates

My Work as a Student

Careers — Work with a partner. Each of you will choose one of the people in this unit. Review the work that each person does. Then compare their work. In what ways is it similar? In what ways is it different? (Think about training, practice, place of work, and so on.)

What are you learning at school that would help you prepare for similar careers?

Character — *Fairness* is one of the character traits Tracy Wieland finds essential in her work as a web site designer. In what ways can you relate fairness to your work at school? (You might think about group and partner work, decision making, sharing, and speaking and listening.) List the many ways you are fair in your life at school.

How can you tell when you are being fair? What feelings do you feel? What thoughts do you think?

Set a goal of a new way you want to be fair at school in the near future.

UNIT EIGHT

I Work for the Government

A Nation's Strength

Ralph Waldo Emerson

Not gold, but only man can make
A people great and strong;
Men who, for truth and honor's sake,
Stand fast and suffer long.

Brave men who work while others sleep,
Who dare while others fly—
They build a nation's pillars deep
And lift them to the sky.

The people described in this poem represent more than 2 million Americans—the people who are employed by the government. In the first stanza, the poem refers to soldiers and others who put themselves at risk for our country. Read the stanza aloud. Doesn't it sound like a victory march?

In the second stanza, we read about the less celebrated workers—those who keep the country running smoothly by doing their jobs day after day. Who are these workers? You'll meet some of them in this unit.

As you read about the four government workers, think about their "pillars." How can the *Pillars of Character* to which they are devoted be seen as important pillars for our nation to "lift to the sky"?

Captain Patricia Johnson

Captain, USMC

In 1980 Patricia Johnson was about to graduate from high school in Milwaukee, Wisconsin. She had dreams of traveling, meeting people, and getting a college education. Her dreams became reality when she joined the United States Marine Corps.

Since joining the Corps, Patricia has earned not only a college degree but also a graduate degree in business administration. She has traveled to interesting places such as Alaska, Japan, and Korea. She has moved up through the **ranks** and now proudly bears the title

“One will always succeed in a profession one likes.”

Captain Patricia Johnson, Public Affairs Officer.

Captain Johnson currently lives and works in our nation's capital. Her job revolves around information—staying current on world affairs, finding the answers to people's questions about the Marine Corps, presenting facts clearly. Fortunately for Patricia, reading is one of her favorite activities. As she says, “I enjoy reading. Through reading learning never stops.” Captain Johnson also feels fortunate because her job allows her to help people. She feels that her love for this part of her job is part of her success: “One will always succeed in a profession one likes. I like helping people.”

Although Patricia didn't have a specific career in mind until high school graduation was upon her, she was careful to prepare herself well from middle school on. In sixth grade she was taught by her teacher that she should never say, "I can't." From that point on, always trying her best became Patricia's way of life. She studied hard so that she would get good grades. She kept a positive attitude. Today Johnson encourages students like you to do the same: "The sky is the limit. Anything's possible, but you have to work hard and never quit."

With Johnson's commitment to hard work, it's no surprise that she selects Trustworthiness as the most important *Pillar of Character*. She summarizes it simply: "Be true to yourself. Be loyal and honest to your boss." Captain Johnson adds that Respect for Others should be practiced daily. As she points out, it's important to remember to treat others as you want to be treated.

Trustworthiness
Respect for Others

Critical Thinking

1. Which of Patricia's dreams has she fulfilled?
2. How does loving to read help in Patricia's current position in the Marine Corps?
3. What important lesson did Patricia learn from a sixth-grade teacher?
4. How would you describe Captain Patricia Johnson's character?

Hilda Gallegos

USDA Forest Service

After graduating from high school in Los Angeles, California, Hilda Gallegos decided to give college a try. After one semester, however, she left school to go to work full-time. The job she took was a **data entry** job. She and about 50 other people worked in a room together eight hours a day, entering information into computer terminals. Hilda describes what she discovered:

> "I would once in a while catch a glimpse of the programmers, and they were definitely having much more fun at what they were doing than I was. . . so I talked with them and decided that if they could do it, so could I."

That's when Gallegos made a promise to herself to return to college and work very hard to get a good education.

Hilda Gallegos kept that promise to herself. She earned a college degree in business information systems. As a result, for 16 years she has had great jobs as a **civil servant**, working for the federal government. At her current job, in Salt Lake City, Utah, Gallegos is a "Fire, Aviation and Air Quality Management Computer Specialist." That's a big title—but then, Hilda Gallegos has a big job. She's a problem-solver, and at certain times of the year (such as fire season), she has lots of problems to solve. For example, she helps people use their computers more efficiently to get their jobs done. When something goes wrong, she travels to be on the spot and correct the situation. She also works to solve problems involving scheduling and training

"... if they could do it, so could I."

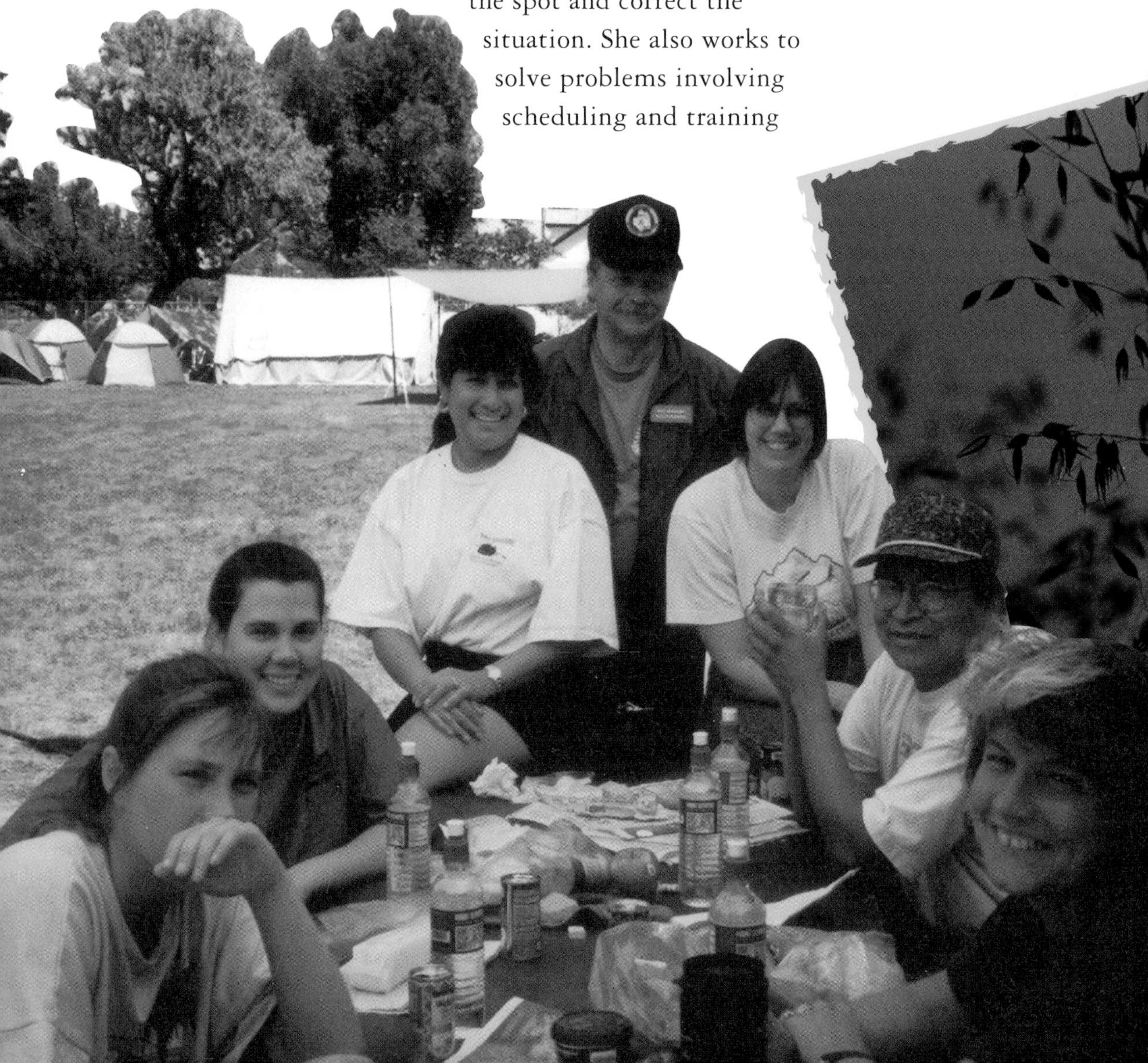

for many computer applications used in Fire, Aviation, and Air Quality.

To stay on top of her job, Hilda is always happy to find and learn new technology. She keeps up with changes because often that's what allows her to best help others. It's when she's able to assist others that Hilda Gallegos is most happy with her job.

In keeping her promise to herself to always be her best, Hilda has achieved success. Her commitment to Trustworthiness shows in her hard work, but it also shows in her relationships with people. As she says, "I believe that balance with and within all aspects of our lives is what truly makes us happy and complete people."

What advice does Hilda Gallegos offer students like you? She suggests that you talk to many adults about their jobs. Find out what they do, how they got where they are, and how they like it. Ask about the good and bad parts of the jobs.

Then, if you choose an interesting career and are as trustworthy as Hilda Gallegos in working toward it, guess what? You might find a job working for the government—and they would be glad to employ you!

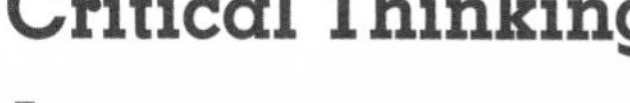

1. What prompted Hilda to make a career change?
2. How did Hilda prepare for her career in the Civil Service?
3. In what ways is problem solving important in Gallegos's work?
4. How would you describe Hilda Gallegos's character?

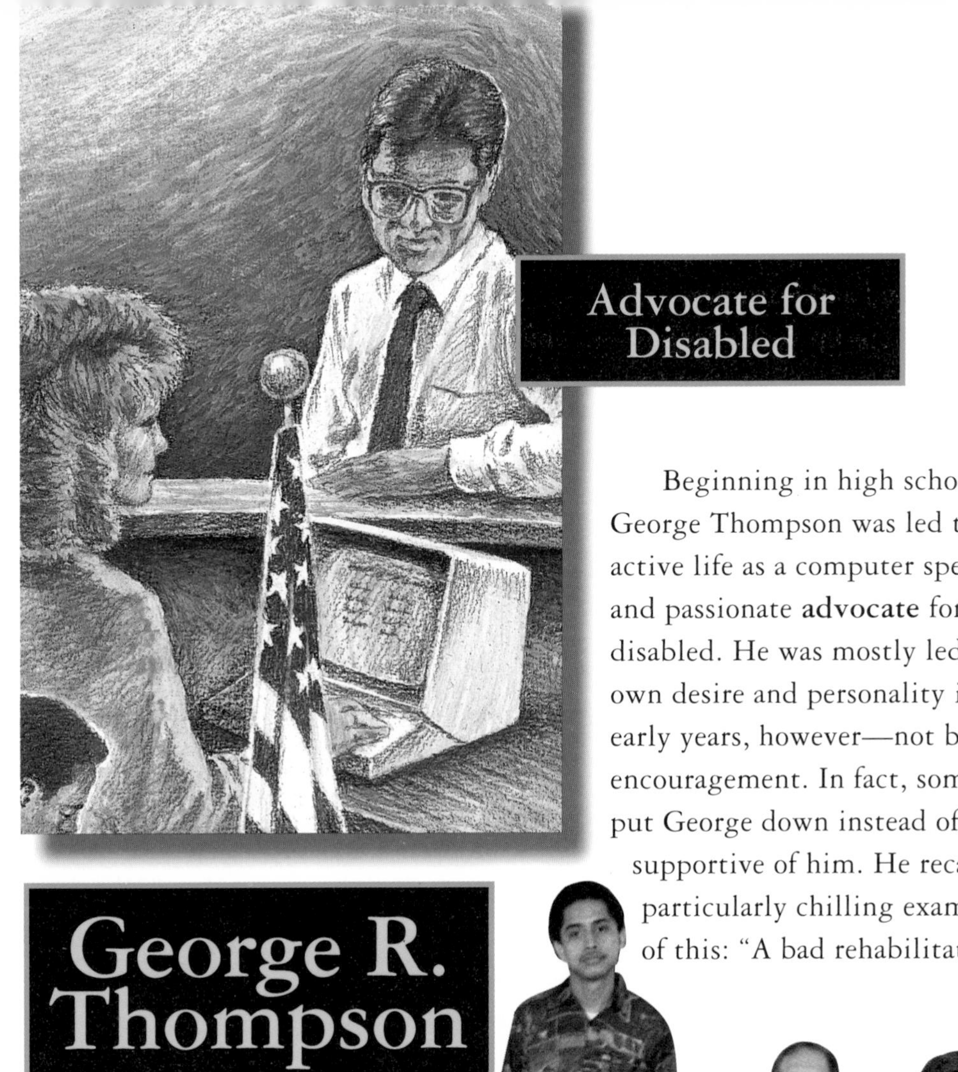

George R. Thompson

Advocate for Disabled

Beginning in high school, George Thompson was led to an active life as a computer specialist and passionate **advocate** for the disabled. He was mostly led by his own desire and personality in the early years, however—not by others' encouragement. In fact, some people put George down instead of being supportive of him. He recalls a particularly chilling example of this: "A bad rehabilitation counselor told me to go home and watch TV, that I would never get anywhere. . ."

Thompson has certainly proven that person wrong. His life is a model of success. Hopefully, through his work, he also has helped to decrease the possibility that anyone will say such words to or about disabled people.

"I . . . knew others needed more help than I did."

Throughout the 1980s and 1990s, George Thompson has been an important force in the fight for barrier-free life for disabled people living in California. He is a trained volunteer for CAN (Community Access Network) and chairman of the Long Beach area branch of AIDE (Advocates in the Interest of the Disabled and their Employment). In these positions, he works to help disabled people find jobs, obtain an education, enjoy recreation, and contribute positively to the community. He also helps to ensure that legal codes relevant to disabled people are met. For example, businesses are not allowed to **discriminate** against disabled people when they hire workers. Public buildings must be accessible to people in wheelchairs. Public services must be available for those who have hearing and visual impairments. George Thompson knows such laws inside and out, and he works hard to make sure they are followed.

Thompson himself has several disabilities resulting from a condition known as **cerebral palsy**, which strikes in early childhood and can affect the brain, speech, and muscle control. In college, his own disabilities were behind his interest in helping others. As he says:

"I needed help myself but knew others needed more help than I did."

Thompson shows his Respect for Others every day of his life. He constantly pushes for government agencies to make respectful decisions regarding the disabled. He comments:

> "A person is not an object to deal with. . . The more you help, the less the disabled person has to worry and can live a normal life like he/she should."

George Thompson, who understands so well the needs of the disabled, is happy to share his knowledge with others. He gives talks to all kinds of groups, sits on many advisory boards, and teaches classes. His victories come, he says, in "serving and getting what the disabled need."

Respect for Others

Critical Thinking

1. What areas of George's work began while he was still in high school?
2. In what ways does Thompson help disabled people?
3. In what ways does knowing legal codes help in Thompson's career as an advocate for disabled people?
4. How would you describe George R. Thompson's character?

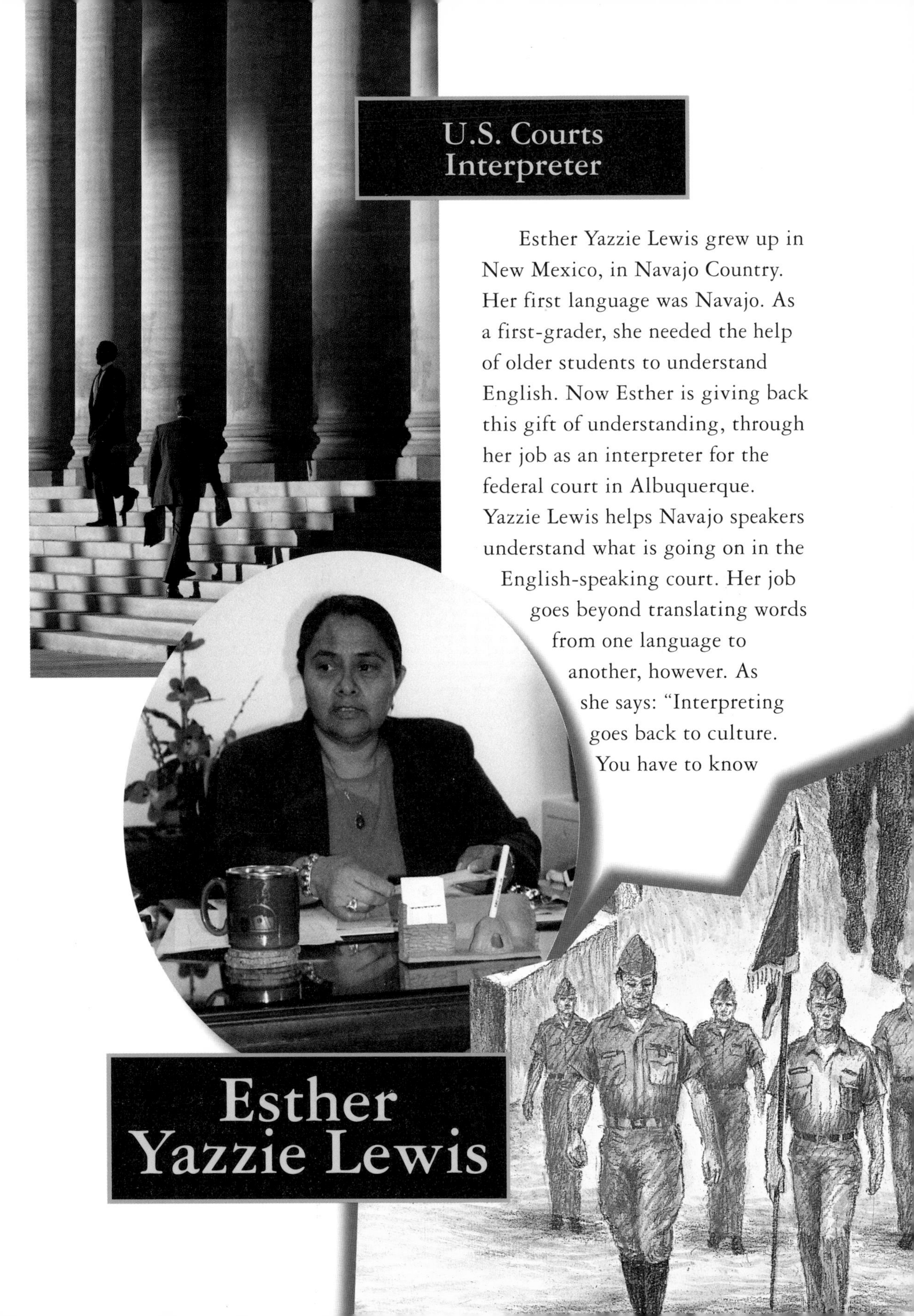

U.S. Courts Interpreter

Esther Yazzie Lewis grew up in New Mexico, in Navajo Country. Her first language was Navajo. As a first-grader, she needed the help of older students to understand English. Now Esther is giving back this gift of understanding, through her job as an interpreter for the federal court in Albuquerque. Yazzie Lewis helps Navajo speakers understand what is going on in the English-speaking court. Her job goes beyond translating words from one language to another, however. As she says: "Interpreting goes back to culture. You have to know

Esther Yazzie Lewis

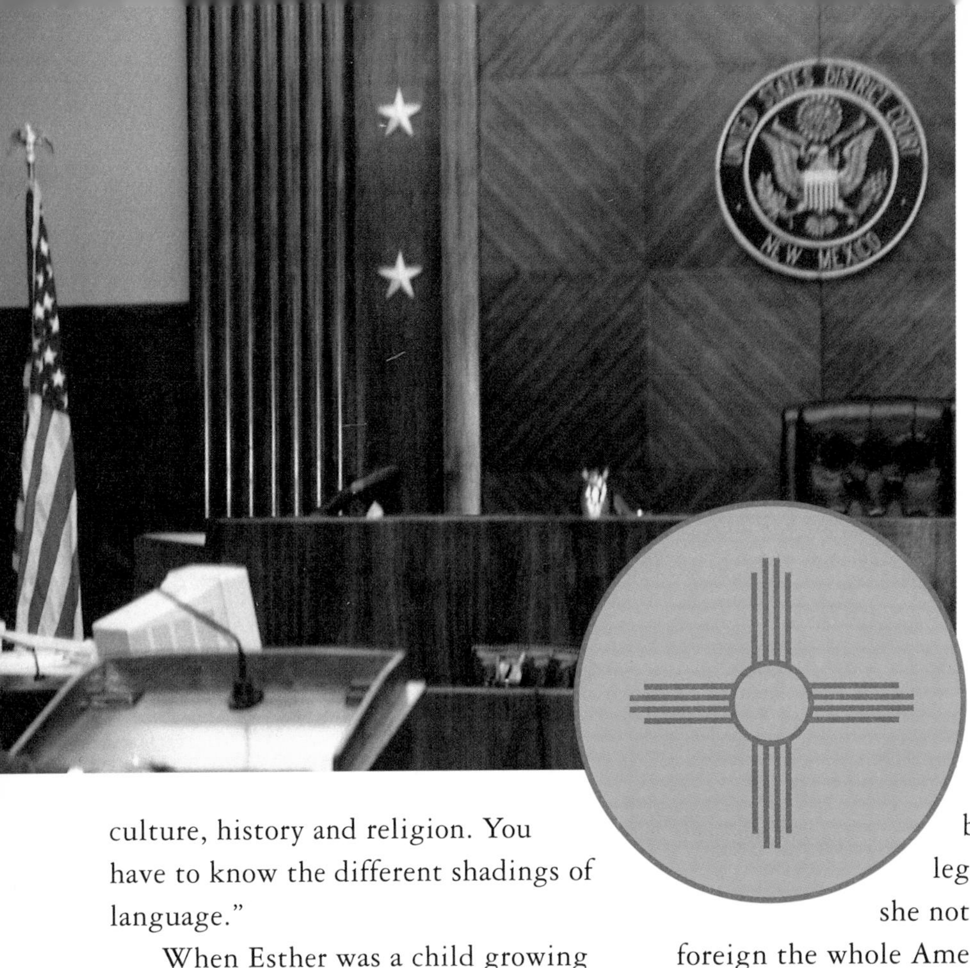

"Interpreting goes back to culture."

culture, history and religion. You have to know the different shadings of language."

When Esther was a child growing up on a reservation, her family stressed the importance of her Navajo heritage. From her mother, Esther felt strong support to pursue her knowledge of Navajo culture. Esther's father helped her to concentrate on the Navajo language. He taught her to be observant about *how* Navajo words are spoken.

The resulting rich knowledge of Navajo culture and language is supplemented by Esther's work experience and education to make her perfect for her current job. In the 1970s, Esther worked with Navajo law enforcement. This gave her a good background in legal issues. What she noticed was how foreign the whole American legal system seemed to Navajos. That's when Yazzie Lewis went back to college. She received degrees in political science and public administration, using her new knowledge to help create a glossary of legal terms for guiding Navajos through the court system.

The glossary has expanded to thousands of words over the years. Still, there is no replacement for a person serving as an on-the-spot interpreter. Since 1990, that person in New Mexico has been Esther Yazzie Lewis. She's always working for better translations and has been known to interview Navajos ("How did you say that? Tell me again.") who use unusual **dialects**. She continues her college studies and is currently working on yet another degree, this one in American studies. Yazzie Lewis also serves as a consultant for different groups, including the Smithsonian Museum of Native Americans, Court T.V., and Berlitz International, Inc. (a company that specializes in tapes and other products of many languages).

What it all adds up to is wonderful results—for the people Esther helps and for Esther herself. She treasures her opportunities to help the Navajo. She feels it is the character trait of Responsibility that has led her to respect and care for people. She encourages young people like you to learn about your culture. By knowing your own self, she says, you will get along better with others.

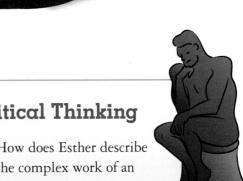

Critical Thinking

1. How does Esther describe the complex work of an interpreter?
2. How did Esther's work with Navajo law enforcement help prepare her to work as a courts interpreter?
3. What other education has been important in Yazzie Lewis's preparation for her career?
4. How would you describe Esther Yazzie Lewis's character?

Responsibility

Group Project

Creating Models of Monuments

Work with a group of four or five students to create a model of a monument. Your purpose is to celebrate the dedication, achievement, and caring of some type of government worker. This need not be a specific person, but a figure who is representative of this kind of work. As you are designing and building your model, think about how you might enjoy working in some capacity for the city, state, or nation.

As a group, come to an agreement about the type of workers you most want to honor. Maybe you will choose politicians, or firefighters, or workers with even more unusual and surprising jobs.

Remember to use your best character traits as you work with your group.

Materials — pictures of famous monuments, including statues, memorial walls, fountains, buildings and other structures; paper and pencils; a choice of materials such as modeling clay, construction paper, scissors, tape, glue, craft sticks, toothpicks, and found objects

Method — Brainstorm about the type of monument you want. What kind of structure will it be? Consider your available materials in your planning. Then draft a number of sketches for your design. Remember that artists often make very sketchy designs using light lines, drawing changes right on top of other lines. Shading shows perspective and will help you to visualize your model. Your finished models should be large enough to have impact, so don't be too modest in your planning. Construct your monument to a person who works for the government. Many monuments have words carved in them—you may want to include a verbal tribute in your memorial.

I Work for the Government

I Hear America Singing

Walt Whitman

I hear America singing, the varied carols I hear;
Those of mechanics—each one singing his,
  as it should be, blithe and strong;
The carpenter singing his, as he measures his plank or beam,
The mason singing his, as he makes ready for work,
  or leaves off work;
The boatman singing what belongs to him in his boat—
  the deckhand singing on the steamboat deck;
The shoemaker singing as he sits on his bench—
  the hatter singing as he stands;
The wood-cutter's song—the ploughboy's, on his way in
  the morning, or at the noon intermission, or at sundown;
The delicious singing of the mother—or of the young
  wife at work—or of the girl sewing or washing—
  Each singing what belongs to her, and to none else;
The day what belongs to the day—At night, the party of
  young fellows, robust, friendly,
Singing, with open mouths, their strong melodious songs.

Thinking and Journaling

What a joyful celebration of people at work is this catalogue of particulars that makes up Whitman's poem (first published in 1855). The workers all sing as they work, sing their joy and sense of pleasure at the tasks that belong only to them. Whitman hears a symphony of Americans content in their work. In one sense, through work, all people contribute to this nation of ours. "The United States themselves are essentially the greatest poem," wrote Whitman.

What kinds of work start you singing? Maybe you don't sing out loud, but when does your heart soar like a song? Some people get that quiet, joyful feeling when doing repetitive physical tasks. Others get it as their ideas spill in too fast to capture in writing. Others get it while gardening or taking care of someone. Might this work be something you could do for the government? If not, you will still become one of many whose work contributes to the whole tapestry of our country. In your journal, write your thoughts and feelings about the kinds of tasks that bring you joy.

A Fable

Description

Fables delight young children, perhaps because these stories are very short and simple. One sure delight is the improbability of the animal characters that talk, especially the one animal who is in need of a lesson. Usually this character is a bit of a buffoon who needs to learn a virtue such as moderation, forethought, tolerance, gentleness, tact, or good taste. And there's usually another character, a wise one who helps with the lesson.

Fables often:

- Reflect human follies in animal characters.
- Teach a moral lesson about human conduct.
- Include just one memorable scene.

Assignment

Create a fable about two animal characters, one of which is a government worker, such as a soldier, governor or other politician, public health nurse, meter attendant, police officer, or judge. Make your other character the buffoon. All you need is one striking scene of jolly folly, a snafu from which your needy character can learn a lesson. Let your writing show the moral of the story. Remember to use the steps in the writing process as you work.

Purposes to entertain, to teach a lesson

Audience children, or your classmates

PREWRITING DRAFTING REVISING PROOFREADING PUBLISHING

My Work as a Student

Pair Share

Careers — Work with a partner. Each of you will choose one of the people in this unit. Review the work that each person does. Then compare their work. In what ways is it similar? In what ways is it different? (Think about training, practice, place of work, and so on.)

What are you learning at school that would help you prepare for similar careers?

Character — *Respect for Others* is one character trait Patricia Johnson selects as important in her daily work as a Marine. In what ways can you relate respect for others to your work at school? (You might think about ways you are courteous, tolerant, accepting of differences, and fair in your judgments of others.) List the many ways you are respectful of others in your life at school.

How can you tell when you are being respectful of others? What feelings do you feel? What thoughts do you think?

Set a goal of a new way you want to be respectful of others at school in the near future.

Glossary

accountability *(p. 84)*: A willingness to accept responsibility for one's own actions.

advocate *(p. 142)*: A person who speaks, writes, and acts in favor of something.

archaeologist *(p. 69)*: A scientist who studies artifacts to find out about ancient times and peoples.

architect *(p. 80)*: A person who designs buildings and other large structures.

artifacts *(p. 69)*: The remains left by people in the past.

attitude *(p. 47)*: State of mind.

automation *(p. 10)*: A system of manufacturing in which some jobs are done by machines instead of people.

cerebral palsy *(p. 143)*: A condition that can affect the brain, speech, and muscle control.

certified *(p. 28)*: Qualified to work.

character *(p. viii)*: The things a person does, feels, and says that determine his or her goodness.

civil servant *(p. 140)*: A person who is employed by the government but is not in the military.

clients *(p. 81)*: Customers.

coding *(p. 127)*: The method by which a programmer tells a computer the necessary steps to take to run a program.

conservation *(p. 63)*: The care and protection of natural resources.

correspondent *(p. 51)*: A person who reports news.

craftsman *(p. 11)*: A person with special skills in making things by hand.

culinary arts *(p. 14)*: The skills involved in preparing food and cooking.

curator *(p. 64)*: One that is in charge of managing and caring for something.

data entry *(p. 139)*: The mechanical process of entering information into a computer.

dexterity *(p. 6)*: Skill and ease in using the hands.

dialects *(p. 147)*: Forms of language that are used only in certain regions or by certain groups of people.

discriminate *(p. 143)*: Show prejudice.

elite *(p. 32)*: The choice part; the best.

environmental enrichment *(p. 64)*: The process used by zookeepers to encourage animals' natural behaviors.

facility *(p. 7)*: Ease or skill.

flexible *(p. 120)*: Able to adapt to new, different, or changing requirements.

hardware *(p. 122)*: The physical components of computers.

horticulture *(p. 66)*: The science of how to grow flowers, shrubs, vegetables, and fruits.

incentive *(p. 125)*: Something that makes a person want to work, try, or do something.

instilled *(p. 87)*: Put into one's mind in a slow but sure way.

insurance *(p. 27)*: The business of guaranteeing to pay money to cover the losses of a person under certain circumstances.

integrity *(p. 11)*: The qualities of standing up for your beliefs, being your best, and showing commitment, courage, and self-discipline.

intellectual freedom *(p. 49)*: The right of every person to have access to information.

intern *(p. 119)*: A student who gains practical, on-the-job experience by working in his or her field.

intuition *(p. 7)*: Quick and ready insight.

journalism *(p. 52)*: The work of gathering and preparing news.

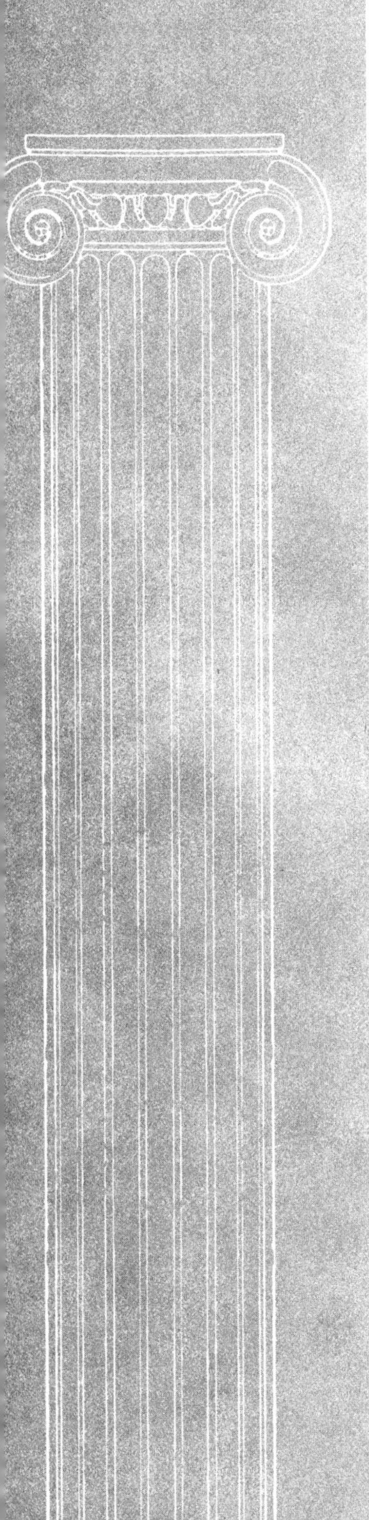

logic *(p. 128)*: Correct reasoning.

malfunctioned *(p. 60)*: Failed to work properly.

masters degree *(p. 25)*: An academic degree higher than a four-year bachelors degree.

merchandise *(p. 33)*: Things that are bought and sold.

nonprofit *(p. 109)*: Not run to make money for the personal gain of those in charge, but to benefit others.

physiology *(p. 13)*: The study of how the body functions.

podiatrist *(p. 4)*: A medical doctor who specializes in the care and treatment of the foot.

ranks *(p. 137)*: The enlisted members of the military.

real estate *(p. 105)*: The business of helping people buy and sell land and anything on it.

refugee *(p. 25)*: A person who flees from his or her home or country to seek a safe place to stay.

retail *(p. 108)*: The sale of goods or products in small amounts to those who will actually use them.

revenue *(p. 90)*: Money that is taken in by a business.

seminars *(p. 43)*: Advanced courses students take in groups.

strategic *(p. 90)*: Necessary for the successful completion of a plan.

summa cum laude *(p. 99)*: With highest honors.

surgery *(p. 6)*: The treating of injury or disease by cutting into and removing or repairing body parts.

traumatic *(p. 98)*: Emotionally stressful.

zoology *(p. 63)*: The study of animal life.

Acknowledgments

Grateful acknowledgment is made for permission to reprint the following copyrighted material:

p. 21: "The Finagle Fiasco" by Don Sakers. Copyright © 1983 by Don Sakers. Reprinted by permission of the author's agent James Allen Literary Agent, Milford, PA.

p. 37: "Arithmetic" from *The Complete Poems of Carl Sandburg*, copyright 1950 by Carl Sandburg and renewed 1978 by Margaret Sandburg, Helga Sandburg Crile, and Janet Sandburg, reprinted by permission of Harcourt Brace & Company.

p. 41: "Freedom" by Wimal Dissanayake, originally appeared in *Kaimana, Honolulu*. Copyright © by Wimal Dissanayake. Reprinted by permission of the author.

p. 55: "Proper Time" by Joseph Joel Keith, Reprinted with permission from *The Christian Science Monitor* © 1958 The Christian Science Publishing Society all rights reserved.

p. 59: "Beauty" from *I Am a Pueblo Indian Girl* by E-Yeh-Shure. Copyright 1939 by William Morrow & Co., Inc. renewed 1967 by Louise Abeita Chiwiwi by permission of William Morrow & Co., Inc.

p. 73: "The Performers," copyright © 1972 by Robert Hayden, from *Angle of Ascent: New and Selected Poems* by Robert Hayden. Reprinted by permission of Liveright Publishing Corporation.

p. 77: Judith Berke "Ms" from *White Morning* © 1989 by Judith Berke, Wesleyan University Press by permission of University Press of New England.

Credits

Photographs

The publisher gratefully acknowledges permission to use the following photographs:

pp. 5, 6, 10(b), 12, 13(t), 14(b), 15(both), 26, 27(b), 28(t), 29, 30, 32, 34(both), 35(both), 43, 46(both), 47, 50, 52(both), 53, 60(b), 63(t), 65, 66, 67(l), 68(both), 84-85(all), 87(both), 90(both), 91, 99(b), 101(t), 102, 105, 106, 108(t), 109, 119(both), 121(b), 123, 129, 137(both), 139(b), 141, 145(t), 147(t), **Images © PhotoDisc, Inc.**; p. 7, 8(r), **Photos by Bill Debold**; p. 8(l), **Photo by Cindy Debold**; pp. 19(b), 39(b), 57(b), 75(b), 95(b), 113(b), 133(b), 151(b), **COMSTOCK**; p. 36, **Courtesy Steve Hawkins**; p. 72, © Shinichi Kanno/**FPG**; p. 92, © Spencer Grant/**FPG**; p. 130, © Ron Chapple/**FPG**; p. 148, © Peter Gridley/**FPG**.

All other photographs are courtesy of the real people profiled in this book. In many instances these photos were taken by their friends, family members, or coworkers. We appreciate their efforts.

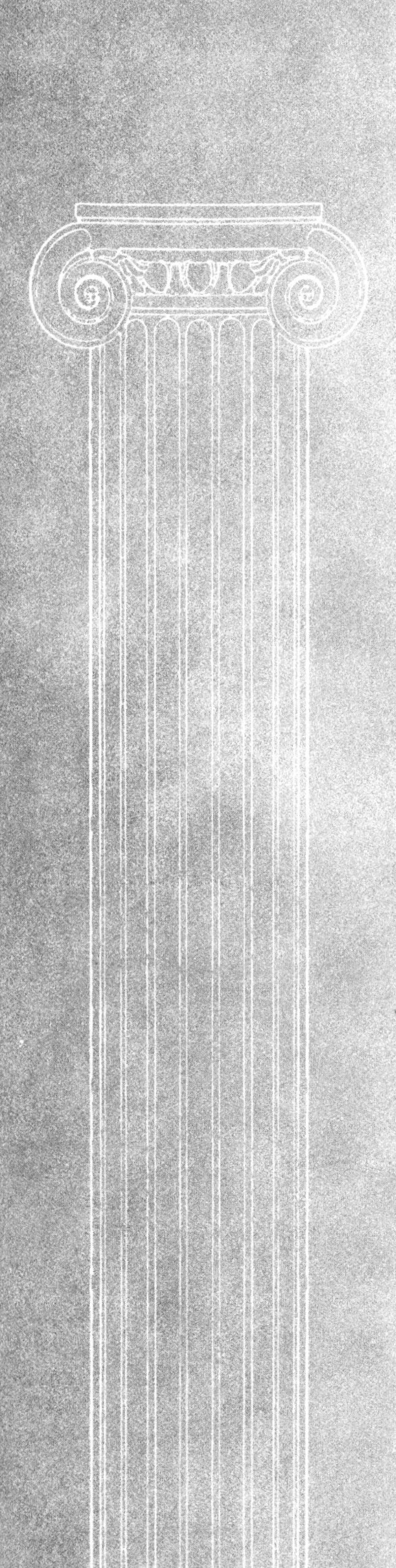

Illustrations

With the exception of the pages listed immediately below, all illustrations within a unit were done by the artist indicated.

"Introduction" illustrations (pp. viii-xv and reappearing throughout book) as well as "Critical Thinking" illustrations: Tracy Sabin.

p. 80(b): David Tamura.

Unit One: Bradley H. Clark

Unit Two: Eldon Doty

Unit Three: Len Ebert

Unit Four: David Tamura

Unit Five: Len Ebert

Unit Six: Bradley H. Clark

Unit Seven: Eldon Doty

Unit Eight: David Tamura